WELCOME

GARDENING WITH EMMA
GROW AND HAVE FUN

A KID-to-KID GUIDE

EMMA BIGGS

with help from her dad, **STEVEN BIGGS**

Illustrations by **ROB HODGSON**

Storey Publishing

The mission of Storey Publishing is to serve our customers by publishing practical information that encourages personal independence in harmony with the environment.

Edited by **Carleen Madigan** and **Lisa H. Hiley**

Art direction and book design by **Carolyn Eckert**

Text production by **Jennifer Jepson Smith**

Cover photography by © **Donna Griffith**, www.donnagriffith.com

Illustrations by © **Rob Hodgson**

Map pages 12–13 by © **Emma Biggs**

© 2019 by Steven Biggs

Interior photography by © **Donna Griffith**, www.donnagriffith.com, 2–3, 5, 6, 7 except top row (4th & 5th from l., r.), 8, 9, 10 t.l., b.c. & r., 11 t., 14, 17 t.r., 23 l., 24, 26, 30–33, 34 t., 35 l. (t. & b.), 46, 47, 49, 52 t.l., 57 c., 59 nasturtium, 62–63, 66 b., 67 c., 68–70, 75 t., 79 b., 83 t.r., 84–87, 90 t.r., 92–94, 95 except sunflower, 96–99, 100 m., 102 t.r., 108 t. & b. l., 112 r., 113–114, 116 t.l., 117–118, 119 b., 120 t., 121 b., 126, 127 r., 131 t. & b.r., 133 c., 144; © **Kim Lowe**, 7 top row (4th & 5th from l., r.), 10 m. & b. l., 11 m., 15, 27 top (l. & r.), 28, 29, 36, 38, 39 t. & row 3 r., 41 l., 51 m., 52 t.r., 53 t.l., 56, 57 l. & r., 59 nasturtium, 61 except t.r., 72 top, 73 b., 78 b.r., 79 t., 82, 83 t.l. & b.r., 88, 89 b.r., 90 b., 100 b.l., 103, 106, 110 t.l. & r., 111 r., 116 b., 119 t.l. & r., 124–125, 128 t.l., 135, 136 t. (both), 138; **Mars Vilaubi**, 17 variegated sage, 55 b., 64 (cosmos, coneflower, sunflower), 65, 67 t., 74, 102 b.r., 128 t.c.; © **Shawn Linehan**, 11 b., 78 t. & b.l., 119 t.c., 132; © **Steven Biggs**, 19 l., 27 t. & r., 40 l., 42 b., 43 b., 60 b., 71 b., 83 m. (both) & b.l., 89 b.c., 91 t.r., 108 b.r., 109 t.r., b.l. & r., 115 c., 128 t.r., 130 t., 134 r., 137, 141 b.r

Additional photography by © Philip Ficks, 1; © ooyoo/iStock.com, 16 t.; © David Q. Cavagnaro/Getty Images, 16 b.; © infrontphoto/iStock.com, 17 basil; © joloei/iStock.com, 17 zinnia; © EvgeniySmolskiy/iStock.com, 17 dill; © Kati Finell/iStock.com, 17 rhubarb; © Skyprayer2005/Shutterstock.co,: 17 variegated mint; © Serg Veluseceac/iStock.com, 19 t.r.; © Mantonature/iStock.com, 19 b.r.; © gl0ck/iStock.com, 20 l.; © Griffin24/iStock.com, 20 r.; © Eselena/Shutterstock.com, 21 t.l.; © ErikAgar/iStock.com, 21 t.r.; © Henrik_L/iStock.com, 21 b.; © Francesca Yorke/Getty Images, 22; © Tassii/iStock.com, 23 r.; © Constantino Costa/Getty Images, 25; © MarkSwallow/iStock.com, 34 b.l.; © Floortje/iStock.com, 34 b.c.; © AlexLMX/iStock.com, 34 b.r.; Carolyn Eckert, 35 r., 139; © Clarence Holmes Wildlife/Alamy Stock Photo, 37 l.; © abadonian/iStock.com, 37 c.; © scorpion56/iStock.com, 37 r.;

© epantha/iStock.com, 39 row 2 r.; © Nature Picture Library/Alamy Stock Photo, 39 row 3 l.; © Voren1/iStock.com, 39 row 2 l.; © Manfred Ruckszio/Alamy Stock Photo, 40 b.r.; © Stephen Dwyer/Alamy Stock Photo, 40 t.r.; © ZUMA Press, Inc./Alamy Stock Photo, 41 t.r.; © Tony Watson/Alamy Stock Photo, 41 b.r.; © MyrKu/iStock.com, 42 t.; © blickwinkel/Alamy Stock Photo, 43 top l. & c.; © dennisvdw/iStock.com, 43 t.r.; © DPFishCo/iStock.com, 44 t.; © Jessica Walliser, 44 b. both, 45 b., 136 m.; © Ethan J. Smith, 45 t., 100 t.; © Andrew Newman Nature Pictures/Alamy Stock Photo, 48; © CathyKeifer/iStock.com, 50 t., 51 t.; © JustineG/iStock.com, 50 b.; © Melinda Fawver/Shutterstock.com, 51 b.; © MarkMirror/iStock.com, 52 b.; © tenra/iStock.com, 53 t.r.; © Nigel Cattlin/Alamy Stock Photo, 53 b.; © BigDuckSix/iStock.com, 55 t.l.; © hsvrs/iStock.com, 55 t.r.; © Floortje/ iStock.com, 58 asparagus, beets, carrots, dill, ground cherry, kohlrabi, 59 urtica, yard-long beans; © ninikas/iStock.com, 58 eggplant; © Suzifoo/iStock.com, 58 fennel; © dabjola/iStock.com, 58 horseradish; © VIDOK/iStock.com, 58 iris; © aristotoo/iStock.com, 58 Jerusalem artichoke; © Creativeye99/iStock.com, 59 lettuce; © popova-photo/iStock.com, 59 melon; © Barcin/iStock.com, 59 onion; © Neil Fletcher/Getty Image, 59 potato; © Jasmina007/iStock.com, 59 Queen Anne's lace; © bergamont/iStock.com, 59 radish; © bonchan/iStock.com, 59 Swiss chard, violet; © DustyPixel/iStock.com, 59 tomato; © AndreaAstes/iStock.com, 59 watermelon; © mansum008/iStock.com, 59 xanthosoma; © stargatechris/iStock.com, 59 zucchini; © GoodMood Photo/Shutterstock.com, 60 t.; Jennifer Jepson Smith, 61 top right, 64 fever-few; © schnuddel/iStock.com, 64 bachelor button; © Westranger/iStock.com, 64 Indian paintbrush; © baona/iStock.com, 64 snapdragons, poppies; © BasieB/iStock.com, 64 calendula; © tbradford/ iStock.com, 64 daisies; © glennimage/iStock.com, 64 zinnias; © Judith Haeusler/Getty Images, 66 t.; © YinYang/iStock.com, 67 m.l.; © Rror/WikimediaCommons, 67 m.r.; © Andrew McLachlan/Getty Images: 67 b.; © Doug Steley C/Alamy Stock Photo, 71 l.; © Garden World Images Ltd/Alamy Stock Photo, 71 t.r.; © Arina P Habich/Shutterstock.com, 71 m.r.; © Martin Hughes-Jones/ Alamy Stock Photo, 72 b.; © Videowok_art/iStock.com, 73 t.; © Christopher Kimmel/Getty Images, 75 b.; © Jack Aiello/Alamy Stock Photos, 76–77; photo by Colin Chisholm, reprinted with permission from Hants Journal, 80;

Additional photography continued on page 143

Storey books are available for special premium and promotional uses and for customized editions. For further information, please call 800-793-9396.

Storey Publishing
210 MASS MoCA Way
North Adams, MA 01247
storey.com

Printed in China by
Toppan Leefung Printing Ltd.

10 9 8 7 6 5 4 3 2 1

Library of Congress Cataloging-in-Publication Data

Names: Biggs, Emma (Emma Vivian), 2005– author. | Biggs, Steven A., 1971– author.
Title: Gardening with Emma : grow and have fun : a kid-to-kid guide / by Emma Biggs and Steven Biggs.
Description: North Adams, MA : Storey Publishing, 2019.
Identifiers: LCCN 2018021360 (print) | LCCN 2018027775 (ebook) | ISBN 9781612129266 (ebook) | ISBN 9781612129259 (pbk. : alk. paper)
Subjects: LCSH: Gardening—Juvenile literature.
Classification: LCC SB457 (ebook) | LCC SB457 .B54 2019 (print) | DDC 635—dc23
LC record available at https://lccn.loc.gov/2018021360

DEDICATION

To Mom, Shelley Biggs, who doesn't mind tomato stains on my clothes (at least my old clothes) and dirt under my fingernails. And to Nana Joanne, who always had the nicest gardens and who I remember when I am in my garden.

ACKNOWLEDGMENTS

Thank you to everyone Dad and I interviewed for this book: John Bagnasco, Robert Chapman, Linda Crago, Cristina da Silva, Owen, Jack, and Tom DeKay, Phil Hunt, Niki Jabbour, Cathy Kozma, Craig LeHoullier, Colette Murphy, Leanne Rabinowitz, Denise Schreiber, Simon Southwell, Jessica and Ty Walliser, and Ellen Zachos. And a big thank you to photographers Donna Griffith, Kim Lowe, and Mars Vilaubi, and illustrator Rob Hodgson, for their wonderful work.

Thank you to the expert gardeners who inspired me: Chris Gark, Linda Crago, Colette Murphy, and my neighbor Joe Pires.

Thank you to Mom and Donna Young for being another set of eyes.

CONTENTS

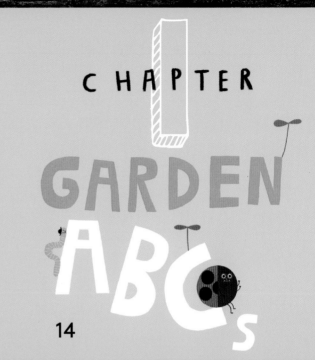

WHY I WROTE THIS BOOK

I've been helping my dad in the garden since I was little. It started with watering plants and making mud stew. I loved having rides in the wheelbarrow, too! From there I helped Dad make gardens and plant seeds. My first garden had some watermelons and cherry tomatoes. When I was in grade one, I gave a presentation to my school about gardening.

Now I have my own gardens — a few of them, actually. I'm 12, so I guess I really haven't gardened that long, but I've gardened a long time for a kid. I love it. And I've always wanted to write a book about gardening. When I was little, I made books by stapling together my garden drawings, and I made signs for Dad when he gave garden talks or had a table at gardening events. When his first book came out, I made signs that said, "By Steven Biggs, helped by Emma."

I've had fun writing this book with Dad. Now I can write, "By Emma Biggs, helped by Steven."

KIDS ARE NOT GROWN-UPS!

KIDS HAVE DIFFERENT IDEAS about gardening than grown-ups do. To understand what grown-ups want, we need to understand how they think. Mostly it seems grown-ups want their gardens to look good for when other grown-ups come visit! For a grown-up, looking good means straight rows, no weeds, and level soil. They want the garden to be tidy. This means they might not want us kids in the garden — because kids can "mess up" gardens. It's about looks.

HERE ARE A FEW THINGS GROWN-UPS DON'T WANT KIDS TO DO IN A GARDEN.

I know because my brothers do this stuff and it makes Dad crazy.

MAKE ROADS IN THE GARDEN
WITH TOY TRUCKS.

PLAY TAG IN THE GARDEN.

KICK SOCCER BALLS
INTO THE GARDEN.

PAINT THEMSELVES
WITH MUD.

PACK DOWN THE SOIL
BY STEPPING ON IT.

STEP ON PLANTS.

LIFT STEPPING-STONES
TO LOOK FOR BUGS.

DIG HOLES
TO LOOK FOR WORMS
OR WATER.

PICK UNRIPE FRUIT
FOR ADDING TO MUD PIES.

PULL OUT THE WRONG PLANTS
WHEN WEEDING.

GET YOUR OWN SPACE!

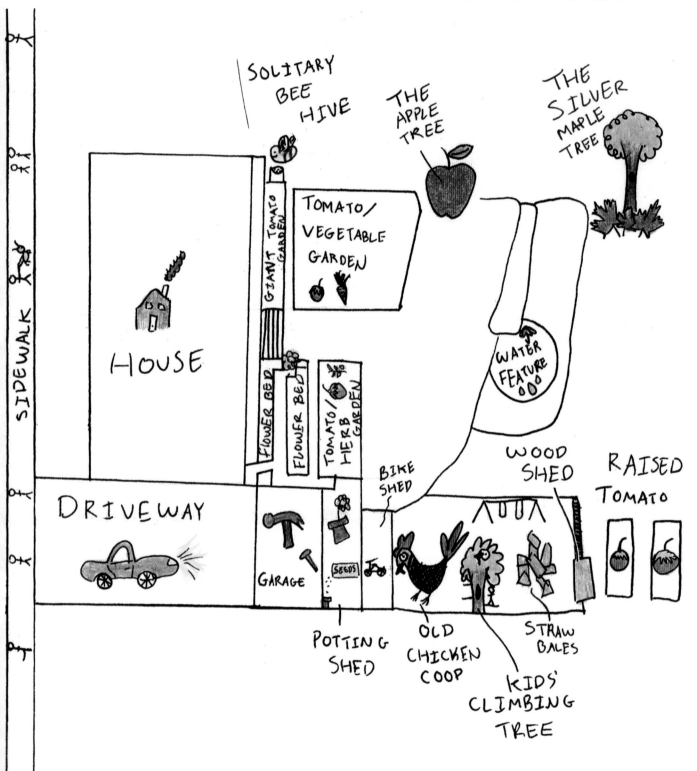

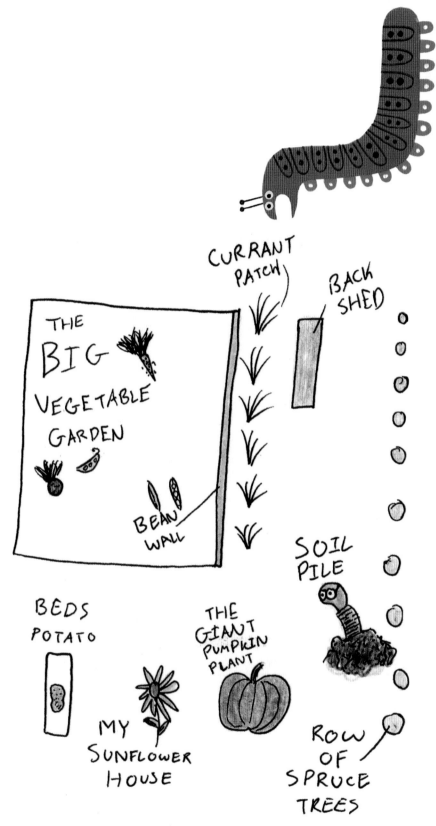

THE BIG VEGETABLE GARDEN

CURRANT PATCH

BACK SHED

BEAN WALL

SOIL PILE

BEDS POTATO

THE GIANT PUMPKIN PLANT

MY SUNFLOWER HOUSE

ROW OF SPRUCE TREES

THE FIRST STEP in becoming a kid gardener is to have a kid-sized place to start planting. My dad used to give me a corner of his garden. After a couple of years, I planted so many tomato and herb plants that he gave me a bigger corner of his garden so I could fit in all of my plants. Now I give him a corner of my garden!

HAVING MY OWN GARDEN MEANS I CAN GROW WHAT I WANT. I don't have to grow "adult" crops. Instead I grow fun things like crazy-colored lettuces and Mexican sour gherkins. I don't have to grow my stuff in perfect rows. My carrot garden is a mix of red, purple, white, yellow, and orange carrots. It's not organized like Dad's garden, but it's fun for me.

I WANT TO GET KIDS GARDENING. A garden is a place where gardeners — that's us — help plants grow. And a garden is a place where there are lots of cool things to do that involve plants, soil, insects, and wildlife. If you don't believe me now that a garden is a fun place, I hope you do after you read about all the neat things you can do.

I GARDEN ABCs

WHEN YOU LOOK CLOSELY

at a garden, you find an amazing variety of plants with an incredible mix of leaves and flowers. They have different names, including long scientific ones that can be hard to remember, and each one has a different way of growing. But kids don't need to know every detail about every plant we grow, just the basics. Our job as gardeners is simple: have fun in the garden while we figure out the best way to help our plants grow.

As you learn about your plants, you'll see how different they are. Some plants, like tomatoes, are sun hogs and need lots of sunshine to grow well. Some prefer shade — for example, lettuce and coleus (a type of mint). Plants like melons and pumpkins take up tons of space, but others, such as carrots, are really small. Dill plants drop seeds that grow into new plants in the spring, but my basil never does, so we have to put it in every year. Some plants, like rhubarb, are tough enough to survive very cold winters, but others aren't. Dad's fig trees don't like our cold winters, so he has to protect them.

PLANTS I PLANT

How many and what kind of plants you put in your garden every year depends mostly on what you want to grow, but also on how much space you have and how much sunlight your garden gets. I mostly plant vegetables, but I mix in some flowers, too, because they're fun.

COSMOS

ASPARAGUS

ANNUALS

are plants that live for just one year. Some annuals, like dill, come up the next season because they drop seeds on the ground that will grow into new plants, but others, like basil, need to be planted every year. A lot of vegetables are annuals. For example, I plant tomatoes and lettuce every year. Some annual flowers I like are zinnias, cosmos, and snap-dragons.

PERENNIALS

are plants that come back year after year. Most of them, like rhubarb and asparagus, are tough enough to survive very cold winters. I don't have to do anything but pick them every spring. I have some perennial herbs, like thyme, oregano, and mint.

BIENNIAL.
A plant that lives for two years, like pansies, foxgloves, and forget-me-nots.

16

BASIL

DILL

ZINNIAS

RHUBARB

TWO COLORS AT ONCE

Leaves that have patches of different colors are called variegated. My favorite mint is a pineapple-scented one with white-and-green leaves.

Variegated sage

Variegated mint

PLANTS I DON'T PLANT

You always find plants in your garden that you didn't put there. These plants might come from seeds that are already in the soil, seeds that float through the air and land on the soil (think of dandelion seed heads), or seeds dropped by birds or animals.

Some plants that grow on their own are weeds. A weed is a plant that's growing where we don't want it.

It's a good idea to take weeds out of your garden because they compete with the plants you are growing. While some weeds are good for bugs and even humans, they might steal water, space, and sunlight that your plants need. Weeds can squeeze out the plants you're trying to grow. It's like having ten kids trying to divide an eight-slice pizza.

WEEDS CAN BE BULLIES

Don't let them take over; every plant needs space. But they're not all bad . . . if you have too many dandelions, you can always eat them. They're pretty tasty!

THREE CHEERS FOR VOLUNTEERS

Plants that reseed themselves are sometimes called "volunteer" crops. For example, you might see a field of soybeans with a few corn plants poking their heads above the soybeans. The volunteer corn plants come from seeds that were left behind when corn was harvested the previous year.

It's easy to get volunteer crops in your garden. Instead of pulling out my lettuce plants when they stop making tender, yummy leaves, I let some flower stalks grow and make seed. The dill and sunflower plants always leave some seeds behind in the fall. In the spring, a new crop grows!

Blanket Your Garden

If you don't like weeding (and I don't), you can make your life easier by spreading mulch on your garden. Mulching is putting a blanket of straw or compost between your plants to keep the weeds from growing. Mulching also keeps the soil moist and saves on watering. I mulch around my tomato plants and over the garlic. But you shouldn't mulch an area planted with tiny seeds, like carrots, because it will smother those seeds.

One disadvantage is that mulch can keep soil cold if you put it down too early in the spring. I mulched a row of tomato plants too early one year, and it slowed down the plants compared to another tomato row that I didn't mulch. The mulched plants had cold feet!

Eat a Weed

My brothers, Quinn and Keaton, and I like to snack when we help Dad weed the vegetable garden. We eat some veggies, but we also eat some of the weeds! Our favorite is yellow wood sorrel, which has super-sour leaves and a crunchy stem. We don't want it to compete with our plants, but we like having it to eat. (Turn the page for more about eating weeds.)

Eating Weeds with an Expert

Eating weeds? Believe it or not, lots of people do it! They're called foragers (*forage* means to hunt for food). When we hunt for morel mushrooms in the spring, we sometimes see people collecting dandelions or other edible weeds. Other people forage for berries or nuts.

Ellen Zachos wrote a book called *Backyard Foraging: 65 Familiar Plants You Didn't Know You Could Eat*. Here are a few of her ideas for kids to try. Be sure to pick far from places where people might be using chemicals on the ground, and always wash weeds before eating them!

Japanese Knotweed

Ellen has noticed that kids often like sour flavors, and this is a pretty sour plant. "It tastes like rhubarb," she says. You can use it instead of rhubarb or cook it like asparagus. She says it makes yummy pickles and is good in stir-fries.

Japanese knotweed grows in ditches, banks, yards, and parks. You can find the new growth, called spears, poking up near the base of the dried stalks. If you can snap off the top of the stem and it goes *pop*, it's probably tender and ready to eat.

Garlic Mustard

Most gardeners hate garlic mustard because it makes a crazy amount of seed and spreads quickly. It's an unwanted plant, but it's good for eating, so when you rip it out of your garden, you are harvesting food! Hold the plant at the base so you pull out the whole root.

Garlic mustard plants are biennials, which means they live for two years. The first year, they grow as a rosette (low clump) of leaves, and the second year they send up a stem with flowers. Ellen says that when you are harvesting leaves to eat, choose first-year leaves or young second-year leaves. You can eat the leaves raw or make pesto with them.

Pineapple Weed

Pineapple weed has feathery leaves and small, green-yellow flowers that look like little helmets. The cool thing is, it smells and tastes just like pineapple! Look for it in lawns and gravel driveways.

Purslane

I pull a lot of crunchy edible purslane out of my garden in summer. It's a low-growing weed that comes up in many places when the weather is hot. Ellen likes to pickle it, but you can just add it to a salad.

Dandelion

Some people hate dandelions in their lawns, but we like to put dandelion leaves in salad, so we don't think of them as weeds. Pick smaller leaves early in the spring for the best flavor. They are a little bitter and the taste gets stronger as the plant grows. Ellen Zachos says to boil the unopened buds for a minute or two, then toss them with butter and salt and pepper — I'll have to try that!

A Dandelion Root as Tall as Dad!

Dandelion taproots are large, straight roots that grow down. Did you know a dandelion root can grow to be 6 feet long? That's longer than many adults are tall.

SOIL –
IT'S MORE THAN JUST DIRT!

You may not think much about soil, but it is really important. Healthy soil helps gardeners. Plants anchor themselves in it and feed themselves from nutrients in soil. There are many types of soil, and different plants need different kinds of soil.

SOIL IS MOSTLY MADE OF THREE THINGS.

- **BROKEN-UP ROCKS** (really tiny ones, called particles)
- **ORGANIC MATTER** (anything that used to be alive, like leaves)
- **MICROBES** such as bacteria and fungi

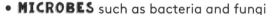
Healthy soil has lots of room for microbes to move around in.

The particles can be divided into three types. Some soils have all three of these, some only one.

- **CLAY** particles are the smallest (smaller than the tip of a pin!).
- **SILT** is in the middle.
- **SAND** is the largest.

The organic matter is the part we can change to make soil better for gardening. Adding organic matter to compacted soil loosens it up so water can move through it and roots can spread out.

The microbes make a community that feeds plants. Plants feed the microbes in the soil, and the organisms return the favor by giving the plants minerals.

CLAY SOIL

SANDY SOIL

A teaspoon of good soil can contain:

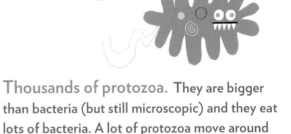

One billion bacteria. Some are good; some are bad. The good ones help break down dead plants and animals to make vitamins for plants. The bad ones cause plant diseases.

Thousands of protozoa. They are bigger than bacteria (but still microscopic) and they eat lots of bacteria. A lot of protozoa move around using a wiggly, tail-like body part called a flagella.

Dozens of nematodes. These are little wormlike creatures. Just like bacteria, there are good and bad ones. Some of the bad ones can attack plant roots. But the good ones do neat things like attack insect pests in the soil. For example, there is a nematode that kills the white grubs that kill grass.

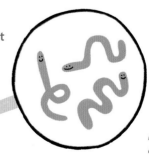

TALL PLANTS provide shade for lettuce.

POTTED PLANTS need extra water.

HERBS do best with lots of sun.

HOW MUCH SUN?

I can't grow as much of my favorite crop, tomatoes, as I want to because we have a lot of shade in our yard. So I have to compete with Dad for the sunny spots that are good for growing tomatoes! Lettuce likes growing in a shadier place, so I can plant it under our apple tree, where the tomatoes won't grow. The main point is that all plants need sunlight, but not all plants need the same amount of sunlight.

Some plants need full sun, meaning sun all day long. Some plants are fine with part sun, meaning the spot has some sun and some shade during the day. And some plants — though not many vegetables — are fine growing completely in the shade.

When you look at seed catalogs or plant tags, look for instructions that tell you how much sun a plant needs to grow well.

These are the usual descriptions.

FULL SUN usually means six or more hours of sunlight every day.

PARTIAL SUN or partial shade is less than six hours of sunlight every day, but not fully shaded all day.

SHADE or full shade mean shade all or most of the day.

Plants Need Light

Plants always grow toward the light. If any of my potted tomato seedlings tip over and I don't stand them up, they begin to bend upward! The scientific name for this is *phototropism*. Basically what happens is that the cells on the shaded side of the plant grow a bit longer than ones on the side that has sunlight. This is how the plant bends to get more light. If you made one of your legs longer than the other, you'd bend, too!

You can test phototropism yourself. A good choice to try it with is bean or pea plants. (See also Sprout a Snack, page 137).

1.
Start a few seeds in pots or paper cups.

2.
Once the seeds grow into little plants, tip over some of them and watch how they bend toward the light. You might have to wait a few days to see the change; they don't move as fast as kids do!

Open and Close

We grow morning glory vines up the railing on our deck, where we can see them through the window while we eat breakfast. In the morning, the big round flowers are open. But by the afternoon, they close up for the day!

A flower called four-o'clock does the opposite. We walk past a garden with them on the way to and from school. They smell great, but what's really neat is that they only open in the late afternoon.

Sunburn a Plant

When spring comes and I spend more time in my garden, I have to wear sunscreen or I get a sunburn. Plants can get sunburned, too, especially ones that have been indoors, where the light is not as strong. Often the nice green tomato plants I start in the house sunburn quickly. Even plants that like a lot of light need to start off in a shady spot so that they can get used to it.

Try it for yourself. Grow a few beans or other seedlings inside. Once the plants are as high as your hand, put them outside in strong sunlight to see if they get scorched. You won't notice it right away, but after a day or two, the leaves get whitish splotches on them.

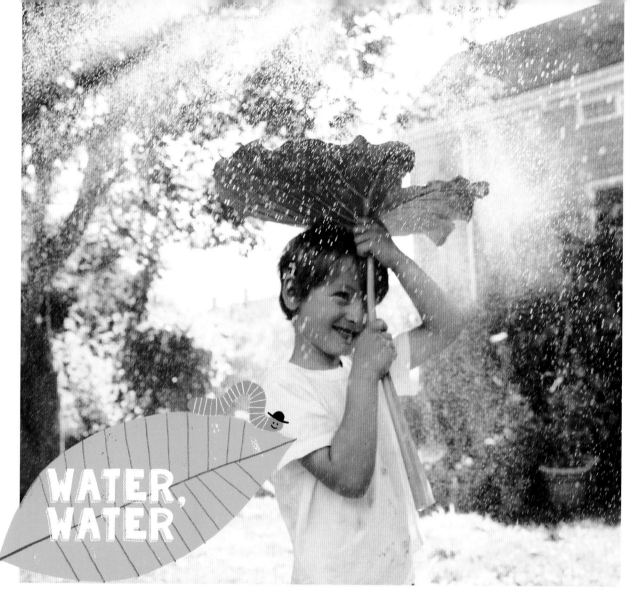

WATER, WATER

I love watering! And not just my plants. My brothers and I love to run through the sprinkler on hot days. And sometimes we fill watering cans and sneak up on each other to have a big water fight!

HOW MUCH WATER there is in your soil depends on what kind of soil you have, how much rain you have had, how much water has evaporated, and how much the plants have used. Some types of plants need very little watering, and some, like my tomatoes, need regular watering.

RAIN IS NOT ALWAYS ENOUGH for thirsty plants. Even if the top of the soil looks wet, dig down a bit to see if the soil is moist. If it's not, you need to water more. Plants growing in pots almost always need extra water, even when it rains.

THE LOCATION OF YOUR PLANTS can change how much extra water they need. Plants near a tree or bush that guzzles water need extra watering. So do plants in the shadow of a house, garage, shed, or deck, where they don't get as much rain.

WHEN TO WATER YOUR PLANTS

If you don't know when to water, use your fingers! Touch the soil to see if it feels moist or not. Don't just touch the top of the soil — stick in your finger to the first knuckle or so. Sometimes the soil seems dry on top but is damp underneath.

If you have a tiny seedling and the soil is dry on top, it's probably a good idea to water. But if you have a big plant with roots that go much deeper, you don't have to water if the soil is still moist below the surface.

With potted plants, you can pick up the pot when the soil is dry to see how heavy it is. Then pick it up after you've watered. Once you know how heavy a watered pot feels, you have a good idea when it needs water.

Dig for Water

See if you can find your water table! No, that's not a place in your yard where you can sit down for a meal. It's underground, sometimes near the surface and sometimes very deep, and is the layer where all the spaces in the soil are full of water.

Where we live, the water table is closer to the surface in the spring, when there's lots of water soaking into the ground from snow melting and spring rains. Dad thinks the high water table in the spring is why fruit trees won't grow in some parts of our yard — the soil stays too wet for too long in the spring.

But one summer when my brothers and I dug for water in the yard, we had to dig to about 2 feet before we found water. (Dad wasn't too happy because we dug where he had just reseeded the lawn!)

A COOL WAY TO WATER

We grow tomatoes, peppers, eggplants, and melons in planters on our flat garage roof. But the garage roof gets so hot that the planters dry out quickly. We fixed that by making planters that water themselves!

MOST POTS HAVE HOLES in the bottom so that extra water drains away. But many of our pots have a hidden tank to hold extra water so the soil stays moist longer than it would in a regular container. I fill the tank through a tube at the bottom of my pots, just like filling a car with gas!

THE WAY IT WORKS is that there's potting soil in the corners of the water-storage area. Water rises through the soil and spreads up into the whole container. It can go against gravity because of the small airspaces in the soil. This is called *wicking*, or capillary action.

TO SEE WICKING IN ACTION, roll up a piece of paper towel and stick the end in a glass of water. The water moves up the paper towel. It's the same thing that happens in an oil lamp when oil moves up a wick.

HERBS
IN POTS

GARDEN SUPPLIES

I love shopping for seeds and finding cool things that I haven't grown before. But one of the great things about gardening is that you don't need much equipment. Here is what Dad and I use.

POTS. We buy some pots, but sometimes we're lucky and people put big containers on the curb for garbage pickup. Clay pots look nice, but they break when my brothers knock them over, so we don't have many left. They also dry out more quickly than plastic pots.

We go through a lot of small flowerpots for growing seedlings, so some of our friends and relatives save them for us. Once, we got a bunch of free pots from a garden center that collects old pots from customers!

SUPPORTS AND TIES. Tall or heavy plants like tomatoes and pole beans need support or they'll sprawl all over the ground. You can buy stakes or use strong, straight sticks. We keep a couple of balls of twine on hand for tying plants.

Tying tomatoes to stakes is a lot of work, so Dad and I prefer tomato cages, which are a wire support for the plants. We buy some tomato cages, but to make bigger ones, we cut pieces from sheets of wire mesh and bend them into shape.

Pots are great for plants that spread a lot, like mint. I have 19 types of mint. I plant some in large plastic pots and some in hypertufa troughs that Dad and I made (see page 84).

When I'm done tying my tomato plants, my hands are greenish yellow and smell really strong. Tomato leaves have lots of little hairs, called *trichomes*. When we touch the leaves, the trichomes break and give off the color and smell. I love that smell!

DIGGING WITH A SPADE

CULTIVATING TOOLS. A trowel is a small handheld shovel that is good for planting. I use a spade (a bigger shovel) or a big fork when we dig the garden soil before we plant. I don't use much else.

CUTTING TOOLS. Pruners, clippers, and cutters are tools that you use to trim plants. A pair of scissors is useful for seedlings and cutting herbs.

POTTING SOIL. Potting soil, sometimes called soilless mix, is a special growing mix made for growing plants in pots or starting seedlings. Garden soil can pack down and get hard, which prevents roots from growing well, and it can contain fungi and bacteria that might hurt fragile seedlings.

WATERING CAN OR HOSE. For my pots or a small area of garden, I'll often use a watering can. When I'm watering delicate seedlings or a patch of newly planted seeds, I use a watering can with small holes so it gives a gentle sprinkle of water. When I'm watering a larger area, I use the hose with a nozzle that softens the flow of the water or the sprinkler if the whole garden is really dry.

TROWEL

PRUNERS

WATERING CAN

I don't usually wear gloves because I don't mind if my hands are dirty. I do usually wear a **HAT** and lots of sunscreen because I sunburn quickly!

CEDAR SHIMS (long, skinny pieces of wood) make sturdy labels for your plants. You can get a bunch at the hardware store and write on them with a permanent marker. They are cheap, double-sided, and last all season.

Most times when I'm finished in the garden, my hands and arms are covered in dirt. I have to use plenty of **SOAP** and wash two or three times to get it all off. Good thing we have an outdoor sink!

CICADA

CREEPING CRAWLING CRITTERS

CICADA SKIN

HUMMING AFTER HIDING.

CICADAS happily hum on hot days. Sometimes you can find their empty skins on a tree — they leave behind their old skins when they grow new ones. The young stage of this bug spends many years underground, sometimes up to 17, before it grows into an adult.

Gardens attract critters, and lots of those critters like to eat plants. Rabbits raid our chard plants, groundhogs gobble the lettuce, and squirrels snack on my tomatoes, which makes me mad. But we also have a fox hanging around in our yard. I saw it chasing a groundhog, and Dad thinks it will help keep the squirrels away. Hurray — the squirrels won't eat as many of my tomatoes!

What we see the most of, though, are bugs. Some bugs we try to get rid of, but others we like having in the garden. The swallowtail butterfly caterpillars that we find chomping on our dill plants are amazing, and we don't mind them because we always have more dill than we need. I could write a whole book just about garden bugs, but here's some stuff you need to know for now.

COOL GARDEN BUG FACTS

LARVAE.

Young humans are called *children*. Young insects are called *larvae* (the singular form is *larva*). Larvae can look very, very different from adult insects.

POOPED-OUT POTATO BEETLES.

The larvae and adults of the three-lined **POTATO BEETLE** are leaf eaters. They gobble up leaves of plants in the potato family. While the adults mind their manners, the larvae cover themselves in their own poop! My bug-loving brother, Keaton, handpicks them from my cape gooseberry plants for me. Thank you, Keaton!

THE EAR IN EARWIG.

The **EARWIG** got its name from the superstition that the insect crawls into people's ears while they sleep. It's not true, but these bugs sure are ugly! They are mostly harmless (though they might pinch you if you bother them), and they eat decaying vegetation and other insects.

THE MISUNDERSTOOD EARWIG

CRUSTACEAN COUSINS.

SOW BUGS and **PILL BUGS** are crustaceans, more closely related to lobsters, shrimps, and crabs than to insects.

Don't Bug Me, I'm an Insect

Did you know that not all bugs are insects? Insects have three pairs of legs and three parts to their body: head, abdomen, and thorax.

INSECTS

Ants

Ladybugs

Grasshoppers

Wasps

Earwigs

Flies

Aphids

Beetles

BUGS THAT AREN'T INSECTS

Slugs

Spiders

Centipedes

Pill bugs

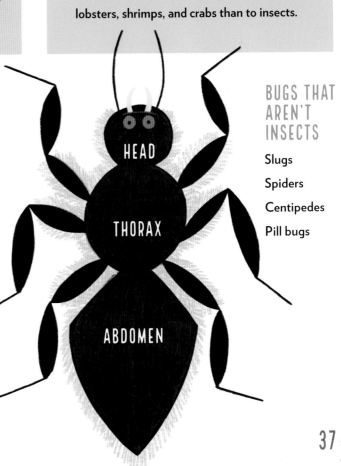

HEAD

THORAX

ABDOMEN

CREATURE CAMOUFLAGE

Find this moth on the tree.

The **AMERICAN DAGGER MOTH** is an expert in camouflage, which means hiding by blending into the background.

EXPERT HIDE-AND-SEEK BUGS

KATYDID. Bright green katydids hide in plain sight from predators — on leaves. Even if you don't see them, you hear their chirping as they rub their wings, like a bow on a violin!

WALKING STICK. Walking Sticks look like . . . you guessed it, sticks. Their camouflage helps them hide from birds, which don't want to eat sticks. At night, while most birds sleep, walking sticks get busy and gobble leaves!

HOVER FLY. They may look like bees as they hover over flowers collecting nectar, but hover flies don't sting. Their protection is being disguised like bees so that predators leave them alone.

MANTID. Also called praying mantises, these predators use camouflage to hide from their prey. They blend in with the plant as they wait perfectly still to ambush their supper!

WONDERFUL WORMS

Worms do a lot of good work in the garden. They eat organic matter in the soil and give off poop called *castings*, which is good plant food. They also make tunnels that keep the soil loose and make it better for gardening.

There are many types of worms. Some make deep tunnels in the soil, and some live near the surface of the soil. You might find both types if you turn over a big rock or a log.

We keep red wiggler worms in a bin in our basement. These worms are great for making compost from organic matter. We feed them fruit and vegetable scraps from the kitchen. They turn the scraps into castings that we put around houseplants or into the garden.

The bigger tunneling earthworms that you find in the garden are good for the soil, too, but they're not usually used in worm composting in bins. They're great for fishing, though. We keep a different bin with soil and some old leaves in our garage, and when we find big, juicy worms in the garden, we pop them into it. When it's time to fish, we have worms ready to go!

WORM HOTEL

RAINSTORM WRIGGLERS.

WORMS seem to hang out on the sidewalk when it's rainy. Some people think they come to the surface when the ground is too wet for them to breathe oxygen, but scientists say they can move more quickly across the top of the soil than through it, and they hit the road on rainy days when they won't dry out.

When I do gardening workshops with Dad, we often take worms with us. I walk around with a handful of worms because some kids have never touched one before. When they see they're okay, most kids try holding them.

Listen for Rustling and Hunt for Castings

WORM CASTINGS!

DID YOU KNOW you can "hear" worms at night in the spring? Take a blanket or sleeping bag outside after dark and lie next to a spot where you know lots of worms live. The worms themselves don't make noise, but on a quiet spring evening with no wind, you might hear dry leaves on the surface of the garden rustling as busy worms move them!

For a daytime worm hunt, see if you can find worm castings in the garden. Worm cast is worm excrement — worm doo-doo made from the soil, organic matter, and microorganisms they eat. They make "deposits" that you can see on the surface of the soil!

Worms come out at night because their skin dries out in the hot sun. That makes the morning, before people walk on the lawn and birds and animals move around the garden, a good time to see piles of worm castings. You might be surprised how many piles you find! Count them!

AWFUL APHIDS AND THEIR ENEMIES

Plants often attract bugs that like to eat them. A lot of gardeners and professional greenhouses use good bugs to control these bad bugs. The good bugs are called *beneficial insects* or *biological controls*. Some are predators that gobble up bad bugs. Some are parasites that lay an egg inside a bad bug — and when the egg hatches, the young parasite eats the bad bug. Imagine getting eaten from the inside out . . . who needs a comic book?

APHIDS. These common garden pests have a body part called a *stylet*, which they stick into plants and use to guzzle sap. It's like drinking soda through a straw, except they guzzle so much sap that they give off a sticky liquid, called *honeydew*, from their back end. No manners!

They're no friend of gardeners because they gobble all kinds of plants, from vegetables to flowers. But other bugs like to prey on aphids.

APHIDIUS WASPS. If you look closely at a big bunch of aphids, you might see some that are brown and papery. Those are aphid "mummies." A tiny parasitic wasp, smaller than a fruit fly, uses its stinger-like body part called an *ovipositor* to stick an egg into the aphid.

The aphid stays alive while the egg inside hatches and grows into a young wasp larva that eats the aphid from the inside! The aphid dies, and the skin turns brown and papery. Then one day, a little wasp pokes a hole through the dried, mummified aphid skin and flies away.

MUMMIFIED APHID

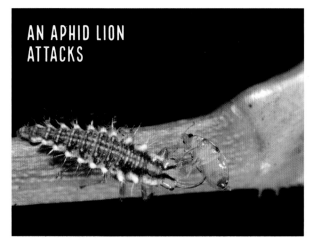

AN APHID LION ATTACKS

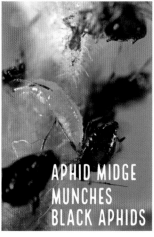

APHID MIDGE MUNCHES BLACK APHIDS

YOUNG LADYBUG

APHID LIONS. These predators are also called green lacewings. The adult has green see-through wings and is pretty to look at. It eats pollen and nectar from flowers — and slurps up some aphid honeydew. The lionlike larva doesn't roar, but this hungry predator roams around and gulps up the aphids!

ANTS. Lacewing adults aren't the only bug that likes honeydew. Ants eat honeydew, too. Ants "milk" aphids, sort of like how people milk cows.

APHID MIDGES. Grown-up aphid midges look like mosquitos. But the orange larva of the midge wriggles around, finds aphids, and injects them with poison before it eats them up. I love seeing these orange jelly blobs on my plants!

LADYBUGS. Young ladybugs don't look like their mom and dad. They're more like tiny alligators! But the whole family eats aphids. The mom lays eggs near aphids. You'll see clusters of small orange-yellow eggs on the bottom of leaves. Like aphid lion larvae, ladybug larvae march around looking for insect snacks like aphids.

KID-TESTED TIP
Baby Gate for Bad Bugs

Cutworms are bugs that chew through the stems of young tomato plants. As you plant tomatoes in the garden, wrap a strip of newspaper around their stems. It's like a baby gate for naughty bugs. Sometimes we can beat bad bugs by blocking them.

Afraid of Bugs? Don't Bee!

Jessica Walliser is a horticulturist (a professional gardener) who wrote a book called *Attracting Beneficial Bugs to Your Garden*. She says 99.9 percent of insects are not harmful to humans.

One bug that looks freaky but is a great bug for kids who are just getting into bugs is the tomato hornworm. You find them on tomato plants. They don't bite or sting, and their skin is rubbery, not prickly. You can let them crawl all over you, and they won't hurt you.

Jessica Walliser's son, Ty, who is my age, does lots of neat projects with bugs. He is especially interested in caterpillars and millipedes, which his class raised. The class also raised pill bugs in containers and watched to see if the bugs preferred the light or the shaded side of the container. Ty and his mom raised a swallowtail butterfly caterpillar in a glass jar. He got to release it! Another favorite activity is to put a few fireflies in a jar with some grass and watch them for an hour or two before releasing them.

One thing I found surprising is that Ty does not like worms. He says he even walks around them on the sidewalk because of the sliminess.

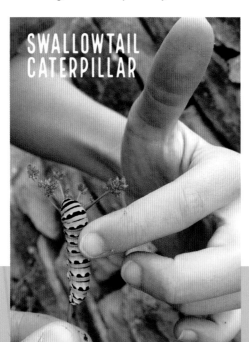

SWALLOWTAIL CATERPILLAR

SWALLOWTAIL BUTTERFLY

BEE ON
BLUEBERRY
BUSH

Planting for Bugs

"People tend to like things clean and tidy and neat, but bugs don't like that one bit," Jessica says. An easy way to get more good bugs in the garden is to leave them a few piles of yard waste or old leaves, and a couple of fallen branches or rotting logs. "That's where a lot of insects spend the winter and lay eggs," she explains. The clean and tidy problem sounds like an adult thing to me.

I asked what easy-to-grow plants kids should plant to attract beneficial

bugs. "Cosmos is one of my favorites," Jessica says. I'm glad to hear that, because cosmos is super easy to grow. It comes up by itself in my garden every year.

Jessica also recommends sunflowers because they have lots of nectar and pollen, and they have a cool thing called an *extrafloral nectary*. It's a part on the bottom of leaves that produces nectar. Look on the bottom of sunflower leaves on a warm day and you'll see bugs gathered there for the nectar. Another good plant is dill, because its plentiful flowers are a good place for super-small parasitic wasps to get nectar.

Ty recommends blueberry bushes because bumblebees love blueberry bushes, and they are important pollinators. They do something really neat with blueberry flowers called *buzz pollination*. They buzz the flower without flapping their wings. You can hear them buzzing. It shakes the flower really fast, loosens pollen, and pollinates the flower.

Vacuum Up Bugs

My brother Keaton loves collecting bugs. He went through two battery-powered bug vacuums. The first was defective, and he left the second one out in the rain. Then it didn't work anymore. So Dad made a kid-powered one that doesn't need batteries. It's a lot of fun. We use it to look closely at flying bugs, and Keaton enjoys vacuuming up tons of ants to observe.

Here's how to make one yourself.

1. Collect Your Materials

* A plastic jar with a lid (safer than glass)
* 2 pieces of clear silicone tubing with a ½-inch interior diameter (At first we used tubes with a smaller diameter, but bumble-bees got stuck in them and were not too happy when we had to blow hard to shoot them back out!) A length of about 12 inches is plenty for the tube you suck through. You can make the "vacuuming" tube a bit longer; ours is about 15 inches long.
* Small square of screen or fine mesh (so you don't breathe in a bug!)
* A drill or utility knife, duct tape, and scissors

2. Put It Together

Ask a grown-up to make two holes in the jar lid with a drill or utility knife. The holes should be the same size as the tubing. Fit one end of a tube into each hole. If necessary, use tape to make the tubes fit snugly in the holes. Wrap the screen over the end of the shorter tube and fasten it with tape. The screened end goes inside the jar to stop the bugs from going into your mouth!

3. Catch Some Bugs!

Put the end of the capture tube close to the bug that you want to catch and suck in through the other tube. Always remember to release your bugs when you're done studying them.

U-Pick Slug Control

Slugs can do a lot of damage in a garden. They eat all kinds of plants. I hate it when slugs get into my tomatoes! I want all my tomatoes for myself, so I asked for advice from Niki Jabbour, author of *The Year-Round Vegetable Gardener*. Niki lives in Nova Scotia, which she describes as slug paradise because it's often foggy, damp, and cool.

It sounds gross, but she says the best control of slugs is hand-picking them. As plants start growing in the spring, she goes through her garden each day for about 10 minutes, picking slugs into a small container. When she is done, she puts the slugs into a big bucket of soapy water. But it's not a slug bubble bath! Soapy water is good for drowning slugs and other pesky bugs, like Japanese beetles.

After about a week, there are not as many of these slimy insects and she can spend less time on it. She still hunts for them but only finds the occasional slug. Niki is

SLUG WITH EGGS

not bothered by slugs all summer and fall because she reduces the population in the spring.

Niki says it's good to pick the slug eggs, too, so that they don't develop into slugs. "They look like little piles of crystal balls," she says. The eggs are just a bit wider than the tip of a pen and are perfectly round.

Keaton *loves* slugs and snails!

MONARCH

CHRYSALIS

Countertop Caterpillars

My friend Grace and I went to a great workshop about how to raise monarch caterpillars into butterflies. We came back to my house and searched in the garden for caterpillars. We didn't find monarchs, but we found a dozen black swallowtail caterpillars feeding on my dill plants. We put each caterpillar in a separate clear plastic aquarium with fresh dill leaves.

And then we waited.

After a while, the caterpillars pupated (see "Pupa" at right). Sometimes, they did this by attaching themselves to the lid of the aquarium. When they were done pupating, beautiful swallowtail butterflies emerged. After looking at them, I released them outside.

I had one unexpected surprise! One day, I heard a strange buzzing sound. There was a wasp in one of the aquariums — and a hole in the cocoon. That caterpillar was parasitized before I collected it. The parasitic wasp grew inside the caterpillar, and the caterpillar died after it pupated. I was a bit upset with the wasp for killing that caterpillar. (Quinn, Keaton, and I named them all, and that caterpillar was Smiley. We were not smiling when we saw what the wasp did to Smiley!) I let the wasp go anyway. It was just doing its job.

PUPA.
The life stage of an insect between being a larva and an adult is a pupa. (The plural is *pupae*.) I guess it's a bit like the teenage years in humans. When insects pupate, they usually make a cocoon or a protective case of some sort. They don't eat while they pupate.

SWALLOWTAIL

WOOLLY BEAR

Hunting Caterpillars

You can grow plants to attract cater-pillars to your garden or hunt for caterpillars on wild plants. Dill is very easy to grow and is a magnet for swallowtails. If you're looking for monarch caterpillars, look on milkweed.

If you find other sorts of caterpillars, try them, too! I collected a caterpillar that I didn't recognize, and it turned into a really neat moth. Just don't forget to let them all go.

DON'T TOUCH THIS ONE!
This is the American Dagger Moth caterpillar, and it can you make you itch!

YELLOW BEAR

WOOLLY BEAR

Setting Up Your Incubation Station

Raise your caterpillar in a clear container so that you can watch it. Make sure that there are holes in the lid for air. Small plastic aquariums work well, but you could also use a large jar. Or, if you want to put a few caterpillars together, you could use a larger aquarium. You do need a lid, though, so that when the butterfly emerges it's not flapping around your house.

Put a label on the container with the date you collected your caterpillar and its name. (I recommend naming them!)

Put in some food. A good choice is whatever sort of leaf you found the caterpillar eating. Put water in a small, shallow container — bottle caps work well. Add a couple of upright sticks for the caterpillar to climb up and pupate on.

SWALLOWTAIL

WOOLLY BEAR

NEW SWALLOWTAIL

Caterpillar Care

Add fresh leaves every day. You can hold your caterpillars if you're gentle.

Tidy up a bit. It's amazing how many small, round balls of poop a caterpillar can make! You don't see the balls of poop in the garden, but you can sure notice them at the bottom of an aquarium. You will also find caterpillar skins! Caterpillars grow out of their skins, just like kids grow out of clothes. I save some caterpillar skins.

Caterpillar poop is called
FRASS!

The caterpillar makes a J shape as it starts to pupate and form a chrysalis. Don't disturb it once it forms a chrysalis.

When your butterfly emerges, it's not able to fly right away. Don't touch the wings because it's easy to damage them. Give it a couple of hours, and then release it outside. If it's stormy outside, give the butterfly some honey or sugar-water for food, and wait until the weather is more calm before releasing it.

Cathy and the Bees

know that bees are important pollinators, not just in gardens but for many food crops, so I called Cathy Kozma to ask her about planting flowers to attract bees. She keeps bees and owns a store that specializes in bee education, supplies, and local honey.

Cathy explained that a bee-friendly garden has a mix of perennials, annuals, and flowering trees. Bees like many common garden plants such as purple coneflower, sages, salvias, and the mint family. I know they love my oregano when it's blooming, too.

You can also let your lawn attract bees. "Leave the dandelions for the bees," she says. Bees also love white clover flowers, which grow well in lawns.

Solitary Bees

One time we were having a picnic on a sandy, grassy hill and we noticed bees coming out of the ground all over the place, but all from different holes. They were solitary bees, and none of us got stung. They're not aggressive like wasps.

Most bee species are solitary, which means they live alone, not in a hive like honeybees. Cathy told me that there are many different species of solitary bees. Even though solitary bees don't make honey, they do something really important: they pollinate plants in gardens and crops on farms.

One of the best things you can do to attract these bees, besides growing flowers, is to make habitat for them. Most solitary bees live in the ground or in deadwood. Some like hollow stems or holes in wood. So have a spot in the yard with deadwood, stems, and leaves and think of that as your native bee habitat.

Or make a bee house. It can be a block of wood with holes drilled into it or a bundle of hollow straws tied together. We have one that's a tube about as wide and long as a soup can, with a lot of holes for the bees to lay eggs in. Dad got leaf-cutter bee pupae that we put in the holes. (Yes, you can buy bee pupae!) I hope they do well and come back on their own next year.

COSMOS AND BEE

2 GREAT GARDENS FOR KIDS

I LIKE GROWING VEGETABLES

and I'm especially crazy for tomatoes. I'm not really into formal designs, but I'm excited about lettuce leaves with beautiful colors. So I guess my style of garden is not too organized and has a lot of things I can eat, plus plants with beautiful leaves. For me, that is fun!

What flowers, vegetables, or fruits do you like? What colors and designs are your favorites? What bugs or birds do you enjoy watching? There are plenty of things to think about when you plan your garden. There are many different types of gardens you can grow. I don't think there's a "right" type of kids' garden. It depends what is fun for you.

Pick something that interests you and then use the idea to make a theme garden. In my case, I have a tomato garden, an herb garden, a carrot garden, and a lettuce garden. But your theme doesn't have to be a garden with edible plants like mine. Here are some different kinds of gardens and some of my favorite plants for kids to get you thinking.

A to Z GARDEN

An A to Z garden grows plants that start with each letter of the alphabet. Believe it or not, it's possible to do the complete alphabet! Or just pick a few letters — maybe the ones that spell out your name. You can have a nice mix of vegetables and flowers, too. (I found plants for *U* and *X* in an encyclopedia of garden plants.)

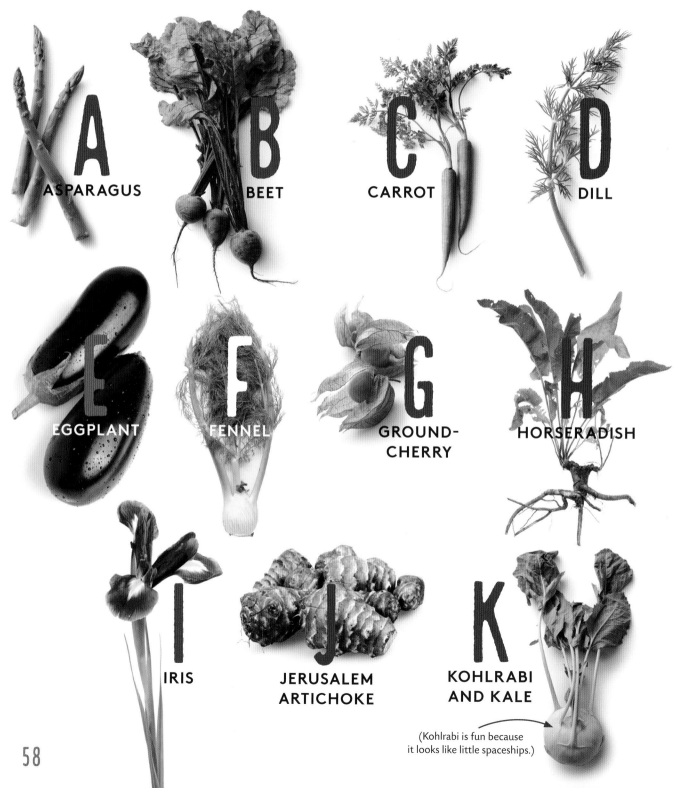

A ASPARAGUS

B BEET

C CARROT

D DILL

E EGGPLANT

F FENNEL

G GROUND-CHERRY

H HORSERADISH

I IRIS

J JERUSALEM ARTICHOKE

K KOHLRABI AND KALE

(Kohlrabi is fun because it looks like little spaceships.)

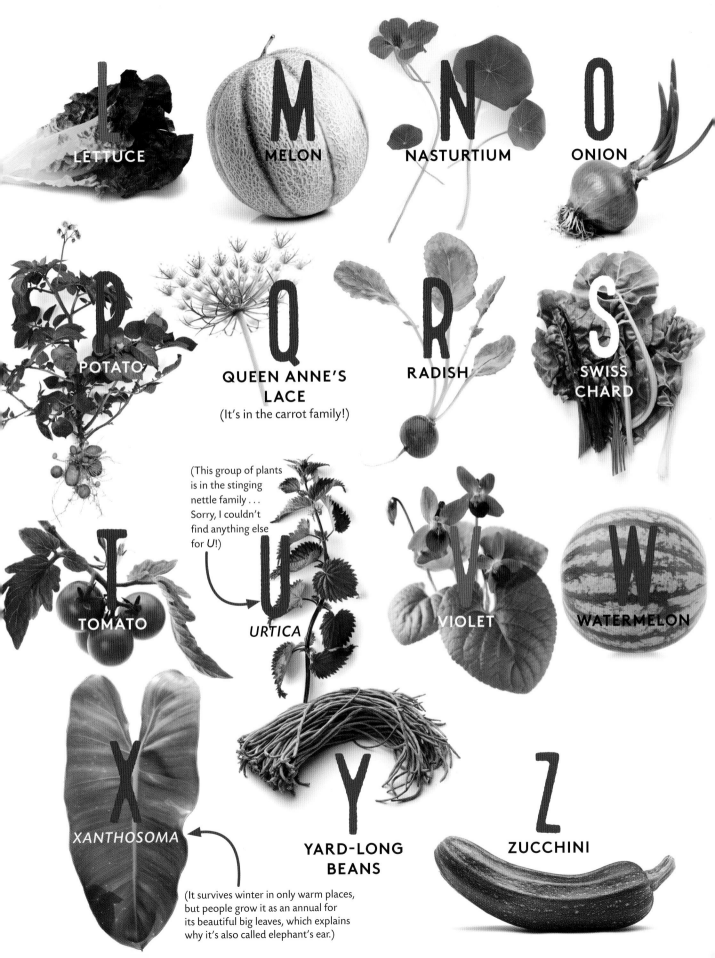

LETTUCE

MELON

NASTURTIUM

ONION

POTATO

QUEEN ANNE'S
LACE
(It's in the carrot family!)

RADISH

SWISS
CHARD

(This group of plants
is in the stinging
nettle family . . .
Sorry, I couldn't
find anything else
for *U*!)

TOMATO

URTICA

VIOLET

WATERMELON

XANTHOSOMA

YARD-LONG
BEANS

ZUCCHINI

(It survives winter in only warm places,
but people grow it as an annual for
its beautiful big leaves, which explains
why it's also called elephant's ear.)

FOR COLOR LOVERS

One of my favorite parts of gardening is how creative it is. You can grow plants with different colors and make art in your garden.

For example, I fell in love with lettuce at the Montreal Botanical Garden. Yes, lettuce. There was a garden with different lettuces planted in a checkered pattern. Some were red, some were green, and some were green with red markings.

Since then, I've grown some really cool designs in my own lettuce garden. Lettuce is amazing because it comes in so many different colors, sizes, shapes, and textures. Who knows, maybe one day I'll be in charge of planting gardens at the Montreal Botanical Garden!

You can grow a color lover's garden with other crops besides lettuce! Tomatoes are great for color. (Have I mentioned I love tomatoes?) Other plants come in lots of colors, too — like yellow squash, white cucumbers, and chocolate-brown peppers.

PURPLE
BEANS ARE
GREEN ON
THE INSIDE

OLIVER'S PURPLE GARDEN

Oliver and his mom, Kim, have been gardening together since he was a baby. He got his own vegetable bed at age three (I like this kid!). At age seven, he decided he wanted to grow things that were purple. Just purple. So he planted eggplant, kale, basil, peppers, chives, tomatoes, beans, and even broccoli. (Who knew there were so many!)

The next year he thought about planting a blue garden but could only think of blueberries. Since he doesn't like blueberries, it turned out to be another year of purple plants in his garden!

RAINBOW VEGGIES

For a really colorful theme, plant a rainbow garden, with veggies in the colors of the rainbow.

RED. Tomatoes come in all shades of red from light red to pinkish red to a really strong red.

ORANGE. You can grow smooth orange pumpkins, warty orange pumpkins, massive orange pumpkins, or mini orange pumpkins.

YELLOW. Cucumbers, believe it or not. I really like 'Lemon', a yellow cucumber. It's about the same size and shape as a lemon, not long like a lot of cucumbers are. But it's sweet and juicy!

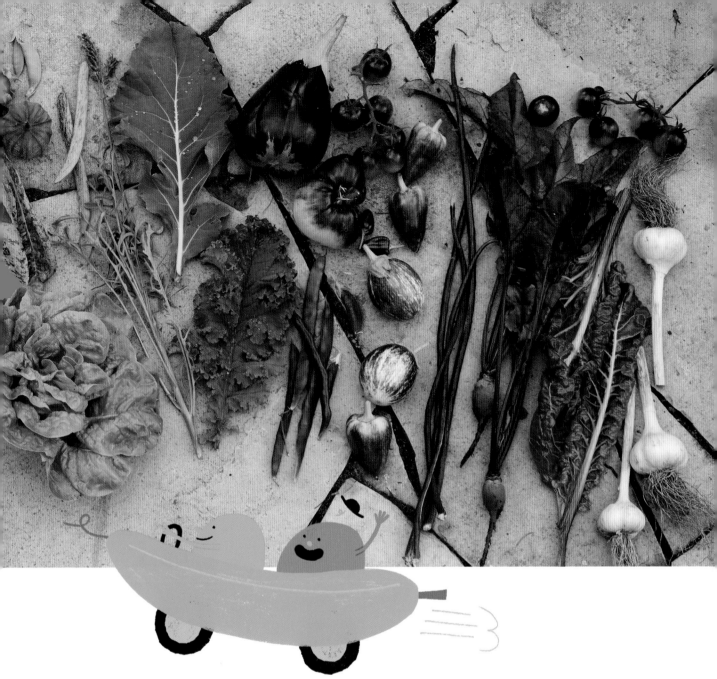

GREEN. Chard comes in a few colors, but the dark green chard with bright white stems is really beautiful. Lettuce, peppers, and peas are other green crops.

INDIGO (BLUE). Blue veggies are hard to find, but I once grew a blue tomato variety called 'Great White Blues'. It's mostly white, with dark blue on the top.

VIOLET (PURPLE). One of my favorite carrots is 'Purple Haze'. It looks purple on the outside but still has orange on the inside. I love how surprised my friends look when they pull a purple carrot out of the ground!

BACHELOR BUTTON
OR CORNFLOWER

COSMOS

PURPLE CONEFLOWER

INDIAN PAINTBRUSH

SNAPDRAGON

GROW A FLOWER STAND

If you love to grow flowers and you want to go into business, selling bunches of flowers might be just the thing for you. Grow a lot of different kinds of flowers that will keep blooming all summer. Plant a mix of colors and shapes, too — you can make bigger and more interesting bouquets if you have lots of choices. Here are a few suggestions.

SUNFLOWER

CALENDULA

DAISY

FEVERFEW

POPPY

ZINNIA

RUNNING A BUSINESS

SISTERS LINA AND ELLA have been running their flower stand, Lavender and Ladybugs, in front of their house in western Massachusetts since 2014. Every spring they plant a big range of colorful flowers and herbs, carefully choosing ones that will remain fresh and beautiful when cut.

Lina and Ella started the business with a loan from their parents, which they paid back in just a few months, and now they are self-funded. They stock the stand almost every day and run it on the honor system. Saturdays and Sundays are the busiest days. After their first year, the sisters made enough money to buy a laptop, which they use to run their business as well as for schoolwork.

Last but not least, Lina and Ella also donate 10 percent of their profits to local nonprofit organizations like the town library and local food bank. Their philosophy is: Making the world a more beautiful place, one bouquet at a time!

To create a bouquet

Start with one or two larger flowers for the center and build around those with a variety of medium and smaller blossoms. Use interesting herbs, too, like the seed heads from dill and fennel. Add sprigs of flowering mint, cilantro, and other herbs for texture, color, and nice scents.

TICKLING GARDEN

When we're picking asparagus spears, my brothers and I like to poke each other with them. The ferns (which grow after you stop picking the spears) are even more fun — they can be as tall as a kid and are soft and tickly and good to chase someone with. That gave me the idea for a whole garden of tickling plants.

AMARANTH. I love a type of amaranth called love-lies-bleeding. It has long, hanging flowers. The seeds are supposed to be edible, but we just use them for tickling and for cut flowers.

AMARANTH

DILL

DILL. The flower heads of dill have lots of small yellow flowers that are very soft. The leaves are soft, too. If you pick a mature dill plant, the seed heads have a different feel but are neat. (Dill is also good for attracting swallowtail butterflies. See Countertop Caterpillars, page 50.)

GARLIC. "Hardneck" garlic plants make something called scapes, which are long flower buds that loop and bend. We pick them off before they open so the plant's energy goes to the bulb. We usually cook the scapes, but before they get to the kitchen they are fun to play with. **WARNING:** You might smell garlicky after a garlic scape tickle fight!

PEA SHOOTS. You can pick pea shoots from the garden in the summer. The tendrils (the curling part that pea plants use to grab on to fences and branches) are the best part for tickling. The other neat thing is that the tendrils are edible, so if you pick them while they're small and tender, you can have tickly stuff on your salad! (See Sprout a Snack, page 137.)

SOME TICKLY WEEDS

HORSETAIL. We don't grow horsetail in the garden, but we always find it when we go for walks in the woods. It has long, thin stems that are made of segments. You can pull apart the segments. They're fun for poking and tickling.

STAGHORN SUMAC. The red fruit of the sumac bush is soft, fuzzy, and good for a tickle. It's delicious, too! We suck on it if we find it while we're on a hike in the woods.

TOTALLY TASTY TOMATOES

As you may have realized, I like unusual tomatoes. One year I had 53 varieties. The next it was up to 68. I grow small ones, big ones, round ones, long ones, and all sorts of colors. Some have stripes. Some are the size of marbles. Some are almost empty inside, like a cavern. Last year, one weighed almost three pounds!

'Spike'

'Cosmonaut Volkov'

'Reisetomate'

'Great White Blues'

'Striped Cavern'

'Banana Legs' (top)
'Kellogg's Breakfast' (bottom)

'Black Cherry'

'Midnight Snack' (top . . . not ripe)
'Lebanese Mountain' (bottom)

'Reisetomate'

'Sun Gold'

'Plum Lemon'

'Moonglow'

'Lebanese Mountain' (back)
'Little Sicily' (front)
'Matt's Wild Cherry'

'Tasmanian Chocolate'

'Yellow Currant' (top)
'Midnight Snack'

MORE ABOUT TOMATOES >>>>>>>

EMMA'S TOMATOES

'GREAT WHITE BLUES'

UNRIPE

'STUPICE'

'PURPLE CALABASH'

'CHEROKEE PURPLE'

Another thing I love about tomatoes is that they don't all taste the same. For example, many large green tomatoes have a kind of sweet and spicy taste. White ones tend to be mild. Here are some cool tomatoes that I've grown or want to grow.

Our friend Linda Crago has an heirloom tomato farm. She gives me neat varieties to try, like these three.

'STUPICE' is a small, red tomato with lots of flavor. It produces early and goes into the fall.

Big orange tomatoes like 'ROSALIE'S EARLY ORANGE' are usually mild, sweet, and have a meaty texture.

'PURPLE CALABASH' has a flattened shape with ripples on a purple-black body. It has a strong, sort of smoky flavor.

Our friend Craig LeHoullier, who wrote a book I adore called *Epic Tomatoes*, grows heirloom tomatoes, which often have interesting stories. Craig named one variety 'CHEROKEE PURPLE' because he got the seeds from a man in Tennessee who got them from his neighbor, whose family was given seeds by Cherokee Indians about 100 years ago.

'GREAT WHITE BLUES', RIPE

'SUN GOLD'

Another variety, called **'MORTGAGE LIFTER'**, is a large red tomato. It was created by a man named Marshall Cletis Byles in the 1930s. He cross-pollinated different varieties until he got something he liked. Then he grew and sold plants for one dollar each, and eventually sold enough plants to pay off the mortgage on his house!

'MORTGAGE LIFTER'

Craig says an orange variety called **'SUN GOLD'** may just be the best-tasting cherry tomato around. He calls it an "incredible tomato machine."

Craig gave me some seeds of a variety that he helped breed called **'FRED'S TIE DYE'**. It's a medium-sized purple tomato that has jagged gold and green stripes and red flesh.

He also told me about the ARTISAN TOMATOES series of small pear, plum, and cherry tomatoes. "They have all kinds of different-colored striping," he says, mentioning red with gold, yellow with red, and purple with green. One of my favorite varieties, **'SUNRISE BUMBLE BEE'** (a yellow cherry tomato with red stripes), is part of that series.

GROW A PIZZA

Try a themed garden with the ingredients to make your favorite food. For example, you can grow a lot of the ingredients for pizza — tomatoes, sweet peppers, garlic, and herbs like basil and oregano.

For a fund-raiser, the eco-club at my school sold pizza garden kits. We took empty pizza boxes and cut holes in the top of the box to hold small pots of "ingredient" plants, which were tomato, garlic chives, basil, and oregano. The kids from the eco-club were running around holding the pizza boxes like waiters from a pizzeria. Lots of people really liked the idea of a pizza garden kit because it was easy to take one home and plant it.

CHIVES BASIL TOMATO

OREGANO

A GARDEN OF SOUNDS

When we go to the North York Farmers' Market, one of our favorite stands sells watermelons. They ask us if we want a melon that's ripe today or one that will be ripe in a few days. Then they tap the watermelon and judge the ripeness by the sound. A hollow sound is supposed to mean it's ripe.

A garden has lots of colors, shapes, and sizes, but we sometimes forget that it's full of sounds, too. Play bongos on your melons. Shake some dried seed heads. Have a garden band party with your friends.

TRY THESE NOISE MAKERS

DRIED POPPY SEED HEADS sound like rattles when you shake them. Find one that has a big flower and a big seed head for your music garden.

NIGELLA (also known as love-in-a-mist) has puffy seedpods that make a gentle rattling sound when dried. Other plants with good seedpods are false indigo (baptisia) and honey locust.

GRASS can make a squeaking sound. Hold a blade of grass tightly between your thumbs and blow on it to make it vibrate.

DRIED GOURDS make good shakers when you move them around and the seeds inside shake.

BEECH TREES keep their leaves over the winter, and if you shake the branch with dried leaves, it makes an interesting sound.

Drag your feet on a **GRAVEL PATH** to make a scratching sound, or stomp on paving stones.

TWO STICKS TAPPED TOGETHER are a good percussion instrument.

CORNSTALKS AND TALL ORNAMENTAL GRASSES AND REEDS make rustling sounds.

WHISTLE WITH GRASS!

DRAG YOUR FEET ON A GRAVEL PATH!

A GIANT'S GARDEN

We love the Royal Agricultural Winter Fair in Toronto. Every November we go to see farm animals, eat fudge, watch the horse show, look at butter sculptures, and see the giant vegetables.

There are pumpkins that weigh over 1,000 pounds. They're so heavy that they put them on pallets and move them with forklifts.

We also see giant 5-pound carrots with so many ends that they look like a tangle of snakes, rutabagas that bulge out like sumo wrestlers, cabbages as big as beanbag chairs, beets as wide as I am, and sunflowers that are twice as tall as a person.

MORE IDEAS FOR A GIANT'S GARDEN

HUMONGOUS ZUCCHINI

REALLY BIG BEETS

SUPER-SIZED SQUASH

OR TRY THESE:
Long, skinny gourds, giant cabbages, massive tomatoes, whopper watermelons

COLOSSAL
CARROTS

GIANT GIRAFFE CARROTS

Some oversized carrots weigh a lot. Other giant carrots are superlong and skinny. The world-record holder was over 20 feet long — about as long as a giraffe is tall! The superlong prizewinners are usually grown in upright pipes filled with very light loose soil.

This creates a perfect environment for the root to grow straight down.

To try this yourself, choose a variety that produces long carrots. Plant carrot seeds in long sections of 6-inch-diameter pipe filled with a light soil mix. You can put the pipe in a pot or right into the ground. See how long your carrots grow!

In Nova Scotia, Canada, there is an annual giant pumpkin regatta, where people hollow out huge pumpkins and race them across a lake.

Giant Veggie Experts Weigh In

Phil and Jane Hunt, cofounders of Giant Vegetable Growers of Ontario, have grown giant vegetables for more than 25 years. Some of their prizewinners include a 7⅓-pound tomato (#1 in the World in 2010), a 222-pound watermelon, and a record-setting pumpkin that weighed 1,678 pounds!

Giant pumpkin seeds can be expensive. Phil had an auction where a single pumpkin seed sold for $575!

Growing giant versions of smaller plants like tomatoes, rutabagas, and carrots is a good choice for kids because they don't need as much time to take care of as pumpkins, and they don't require as much space. But Phil thinks giant pumpkin plants are a great family project. He says it's really exciting to watch. "The first year we grew ours, it went to 500 pounds. It looked like we had an orange Volkswagen in our garden!" he says.

Profitable Pumpkins

Simon Southwell started growing giant pumpkins at the age of 7. His first year he grew one that was 150 pounds and one that was 311 pounds. His largest pumpkin so far was 933 pounds. "Every summer I hope for a bigger pumpkin," he says. He's aiming to get into the 1,000-pound club at the Giant Vegetable Growers Association of Ontario.

Simon has turned his hobby into a business. He sells the giant pumpkins to grocery stores for fall displays. Simon donates a portion of his profits to a local food bank and puts some into a savings plan. He spends a lot of time in his pumpkin patch, weeding, watering, and tending his plants. Once the pumpkins start to grow on the plant, he gives them a lot of water, sometimes twice a day: about 25 gallons (100 liters) every time.

The 2016 world-champion pumpkin was grown in Belgium. It weighed 2,624 pounds — 300 pounds more than the previous world record!

For kids wanting to try giant pumpkins at home, Simon says you'll need a patch of ground at least 10 feet by 10 feet. Along with lots of water, pumpkins like lots of sun and heat. Simon covers his vines with soil wherever there is a leaf, which allows the plant to grow extra roots into the soil. And don't forget the fun part: taking your pumpkin to a local fair in the fall!

Simon Southwell

USE YOUR OLD
RAINBOOTS
(DON'T USE YOUR BROTHER'S
BOOTS, THOUGH)

82

COOL CONTAINERS

MY PLANTERS ON THE ROOF

You can grow a garden in pots and planters even if you don't have a yard. If you make your own planters, you can be creative! Pretty much anything that holds soil but allows water to drain from the bottom could work. What about a worn-out suitcase or a bushel basket or an old wheelbarrow? (You might have to drill drainage holes in some of them.)

Dad joked with the neighbors about growing flowers in an old toilet, but Mom wouldn't let him.

A BUSHEL BASKET

A MILK CRATE

AN OLD DRAINPIPE

AN OLD TOY
(THIS ONE IS EASY TO MOVE)

HYPERTUFA
IS A KIND OF
CONCRETE.

Pots That Rock!

Hypertufa looks like concrete, but it is much lighter and can take a knock. I think hypertufa looks nicer than plastic.

Making your own pots out of hypertufa is a fun project you can do over the winter. Concrete is made with cement, sand, and gravel. When you make hypertufa, you change the recipe and use light ingredients such as peat moss instead of the sand and gravel, which gives you something that looks a bit like concrete or stone, but is lighter.

Other common ingredients are things that you find in potting soils, like perlite and vermiculite. If you search online, you will find tons of recipes. I like this recipe because it is really easy — we just mix cement with the potting soil we have on hand!

Like with concrete, you can build a wooden frame that you fill with the wet hypertufa mix. Once it has dried, you remove the frame. We did this once, but it is a lot of work to make a frame. You need to make both an outer frame and an inner frame. An easier way to make hypertufa containers is to use two pots. Use the larger pot for the outside form and the smaller pot for the inside.

MATERIALS

* 2 clean plant pots, one small enough to fit inside the other (We used a 13-inch pot and a 12-inch one.)

* Cooking spray (or some cooking oil and an old paintbrush)

* A large container and tools for mixing (We used our old wheelbarrow and a couple of shovels.)

* A bucket or other container for measuring

* Trowel

* 1 part peat-based potting soil (The potting soil we used also had perlite, which looks like little white balls. It's actually bits of volcanic rock.)

* 1 part Portland cement

* Rubber gloves (NOTE: Wet cement irritates the skin, so wear these!)

* Water

Project continues on next page

Hypertufa How-To

1.

Spray the parts of the pots that the hypertufa will touch with cooking spray (or brush with cooking oil). This prevents sticking and makes it easier to slide the molded hypertufa out of the pots once it is dry. Mix together the potting soil and Portland cement.

2.

Add enough water so that the mixture is completely wet, but not soupy. Put about 1 inch of hypertufa at the bottom of the larger pot. This makes the bottom of your hypertufa pot.

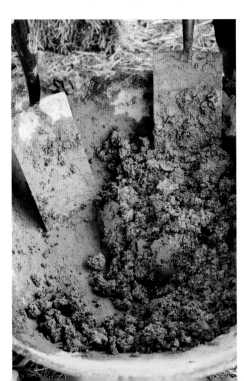

3.

Put the smaller pot on top of the layer of hypertufa, and center it so that there is an equal space all around the sides. Now start to fill up that space with your hypertufa mix with a trowel, adding a bit at a time. The idea is to make sure there are no big air pockets. But you don't want to pack it down too much, or the mix will be too dense.

4.

Fill to the top of the pots and smooth out the edge. Cover the whole setup with a sheet of plastic and put it in a dry, shady spot.

Wash out the container and tools you used to mix your hypertufa quickly, before it dries onto them.

5.

Let the hypertufa sit in the pots for at least a week. It will feel hard after a day or two, but it gets stronger the longer it sits, and the color gets a bit lighter. When it's ready, peel the inner pot away from the sides and pull it out.

6.

Turn the larger pot over and push gently from the bottom. Your new hypertufa pot should slide right out! Drill a hole in the bottom for drainage, and you are all set to plant.

CHIOGGIA BEET

(pronounced kee-OH-gee-uh), also known as the candy cane or candy stripe beet

WEIRD AND WONDERFUL "WOW!" GARDEN

My very favorite type of themed garden is an unusual-edible-plant garden. Dad and I call them **"WOW" CROPS**. These are cool edible plants that are very big or super small, have strange colors, or have a unique taste. They are unusual, like little round carrots or a jalapeño pepper that isn't hot. (Yes, I've grown that pepper, and I took it to school to show my friends. "Hey, look, I'm eating a jalapeño pepper!" I told them.)

I LOVE COOL CROPS, SO THIS IS THE GARDEN FOR ME.
Here are some of my favorites.

DIFFERENT SHAPES.
Check out round carrots, sausage-shaped tomatoes, or strawberry popcorn, which has small ears of red-colored corn that look like big strawberries! Romanesco broccoli looks like an alien vegetable.

UNEXPECTED COLORS.
Look for yellow watermelons or raspberries, or purple potatoes or asparagus, or white zucchini or cucumbers.

ROUND CARROTS

GOOSEBERRIES

UNUSUAL FRUIT.
I love gooseberries, which you don't usually see in the grocery store. They're sour and sweet at the same time. Quinn, Keaton, and I eat them right off the bush.

WHITE ZUCCHINI

YELLOW RASPBERRIES

Super-Fun Seed Selection

Every year I experiment with cool-colored veggies or unusual plants. One way I find out about new varieties is at an event called "Seedy Saturdays." You can take seeds to swap, or buy some from small producers who specialize in unusual and heirloom varieties. One of my Seedy Saturday friends is Colette Murphy, who grows her own seeds for her company called Urban Harvest. She has so many great ideas. Here are some fun plants that she recommends.

'YIN YANG' BEAN. If you pick these as fresh green beans, they don't look unusual. But if you let them mature into shelling beans (the kind where you get rid of the pods), they have very interesting seeds. Half the seed is black with a white dot and half is white with a black dot.

GROUND-CHERRY. This small round golden fruit is covered in a paper husk. It's fun to unwrap — and perfect for school lunches. They're called ground-cherries because they fall to the ground when they're ready to eat. "We just scoop up what's fallen under the plant," says Colette.

'ROYALTY PURPLE POD' BEAN. Here's a bean that changes color: it's purple when you pick it, but turns green when you cook it!

'JAUNE ET VERTE' SUMMER SQUASH. Green with yellow stripes, and shaped like a flying saucer, this is about the neatest-looking summer squash around. "It's super tasty, too," says Colette.

'EASTER EGG' RADISH. These beautiful radishes come up a mix of purple, pink, red, and white.

'BLAUWSCHOKKERS' BLUE PODDED PEA. This pea has purple pods and pink-and-purple flowers.

'LADY GODIVA' PUMPKIN. Orange with dark green stripes. "If you buy pumpkin seeds to eat at the store, it would be from a variety like this," Colette told us, explaining that it has a "naked" seed, which means there's no shell on it. She says this is also the sort of pumpkin seed that is used to make pumpkin oil.

MAKE A PLAY SPACE

I'm lucky to have a great climbing tree in my backyard. It's a big spruce with branches around it that go up like steps. My brothers and I love to hang out in the tree with our friends. When we're in the tree, we spy on adults, play games like tag, or maybe tie a rope to another tree and pull ourselves across upside down, like a sloth. The tree is our kids-only zone.

We make other parts of the garden fun for playing, too. Here are a few projects I like.

GARDEN PATHWAYS

My brothers and I like to play a game called Alligator Water that uses all the pathways through the garden. The goal is to stay away from the imaginary alligators, and the water is anywhere that's not a pathway. Where there's no pathway, we use boards, logs, pots, or whatever we can find to move around the yard. One pathway leads to the vegetable garden so we can collect food to eat in our fort!

BEAN TEEPEE

A fun fort you can make in the garden is a bean teepee. Collect tall sticks or branches and lean them together. Or use bamboo poles. Tie the top. Try growing different types of climbing beans (like purple beans or scarlet runner beans) or vining flowers (like morning glory) up your teepee. The plants fill in the spaces between the sticks and make your teepee more private inside. But don't forget to leave an opening so you can get into your hiding place!

MORNING GLORY

SUNFLOWER HOUSE

Instead of having a fence around your garden, grow tall sunflowers to create a wall. Inside the fort, where the giant sunflowers block out the sun, put a straw floor with a few logs to sit on. Around the outside, grow some vegetables like Mexican sour gherkins and peppers for snacking.

I grew wispy broom corn plants around the entrance where I wanted the wall of plants to be a bit thicker. Don't forget, sunflowers come in a bunch of colors besides yellow!

Broom corn plants made into a wispy broom

Make a private space by planting tall sunflowers in a square or circle.

CARDINAL

BUMBLEBEE

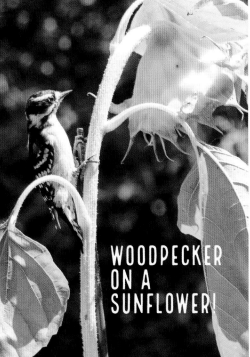

WOODPECKER ON A SUNFLOWER!

BIRDS, BEES, AND BUTTERFLIES

Gardens may attract kids and bugs, but they attract lots of other creatures, too. The squirrels around here love Dad's figs, my tomatoes, my brother Keaton's melons . . . just about everything, in fact. I don't recommend planting a garden just to attract squirrels. But if you enjoy nature, it's fun to grow plants that attract different creatures and then wait and see what comes to investigate. Here are some ways to attract different flying creatures to your garden.

JEZEBEL BUTTERFLY

PLAN YOUR GARDEN

Figure out how many bales you need for your garden and where you want to put them. One bale is big enough for two tomato, squash, or pepper plants, or for several bean plants. You can use them to create a new raised bed or put them along the edge of a garden that's already there. Set the bales out about two weeks before you want to plant them. It doesn't matter if the strings that hold the bale together are on the side or the top.

PREPARE THE BALES

If you are using new bales, you want them to be wet throughout and starting to decompose before you plant into them. Water them well and sprinkle them with a high-nitrogen fertilizer such as a lawn fertilizer or blood meal. Do this three or four times over a two-week period, adding lots of water to the bales each time. The nitrogen feeds the microbes that help decompose the straw. (Nitrogen is the first of the three numbers that is shown on a fertilizer package; for example, blood meal is 12-0-0.)

In his book *Growing Vegetables in Straw Bales*, Craig LeHoullier says that he uses a thermometer to help him decide when bales have started to break down enough so that he can plant in them. Bale temperature, he says, is often in the 80°F (27°C) range to start with, but as you add fertilizer, it can rise to 120°F (49°C) after a few days. As it falls back below 80°F, your bales are ready to plant.

PLANT THE BALES

Mix some garden soil with some soilless mix. Straight garden soil might pack down too much in the bale. To transplant a seedling into a bale, use a trowel to make a hole in the bale big enough for the roots, put in the plant, and fill in around it with soil mix.

To plant seeds directly in the bale, spread a 3-inch layer of soil mix on top of the bale and plant your seeds into it.

CARE FOR THE PLANTS

The straw doesn't have a lot of food for your plants, so you need to feed your bale-garden regularly with a balanced fertilizer. Bales can dry out quickly in hot, dry weather. Check often to see if you need to water. If you're not sure, stick your finger right into the bale to see if it feels moist inside.

You might get surprise guests! We had some interesting mushrooms appear once. They were not edible, but they were nice to look at.

A straw bale is like a big sponge that absorbs water and anchors your plants.

We use last year's bales that have already started decomposing so we don't have to wait long to plant.

We use bales for beans and summer squash.

GARDEN ON STRAW

Our biggest, sunniest garden area has nice soil, but tomato plants won't grow there because our neighbor has a huge black walnut tree, and black walnut trees give off a toxin called juglone in the soil. So one year Dad and I tried growing some tomatoes in straw bales above the soil so the plants wouldn't absorb the toxin. Unfortunately, our experiment failed because those tomato roots went through the bales into the soil.

Gardening in a straw bale is like gardening in a big block of compost! Here's how to set up an above-ground garden.

STRAW BALES ARE GREAT FOR PLAY

Straw is the dried stems of grain plants after the grain has been removed. It's usually made from wheat, barley, rye, or oat plants. It isn't nutritious like hay, so farmers use it for animal bedding, but in the garden it's great for mulch and pathways. (Hay is often made of dried grasses that animals can eat when fresh grass isn't around. It's not good to use for mulch, because it has seeds that might sprout and grow a whole crop where you don't want it.)

Sometimes my dad buys a couple dozen straw bales that we use to build walls, forts, and pyramids for hiding and climbing. In winter, you can pack snow around them for snow forts.

The great thing about straw is that as the bales break apart, we spread the loose straw on the garden and pathways. They're like giant biodegradable Lego blocks!

GOLDFINCH

HUMMINGBIRDS

The first time I saw hummingbirds was when we were at a camp outfitter to rent canoes. There was a long porch with a lot of feeders filled with liquid instead of seeds. Hummingbirds were zooming around and then hovering like little helicopters while they drank the sweet nectar. One got mad at another hummingbird and chased it away. That got me interested in hummingbirds and now I grow plants to attract them.

I grow a pineapple sage (the leaves smell like pineapple) with spiky red flowers. There's also a cardinal sage, and 'Honey Melon' sage with red flowers. But I think the hummingbirds' favorite in our garden is 'Black and Blue' sage, which has dark blue flowers.

Our newest plant for attracting hummingbirds is called lion's ear. It grows taller than Dad! The orange, tubular flowers attract hummingbirds. Because it's up high, the hummingbirds are easy for us to see — they're not hidden by other plants.

Don't forget to place your hummingbird plants where you can see them. We plant ours so we can watch the birds from our dining room table.

FINCHES

Goldfinches are a yellow-and-black songbird. They are one of the more colorful birds around here. They come to our yard to eat seeds and leaves. We catch them divebombing the chard leaves in early summer, trying to snatch pieces. We plant extra chard because my brother Quinn loves watching the finches. Later in summer, when flowers go to seed, the finches are busy swooping in to eat cosmos, purple coneflower, lettuce, and bachelor's button seeds.

HUMMINGBIRD

MONARCH
ON A ZINNIA

BLUE JAYS

My brother Quinn's favorite bird is the blue jay. Acorns are supposed to attract blue jays, but we don't have an oak tree. So we put out feed for them instead. Dad made Quinn a bird feeder for his birthday one year. If we want the blue jays to come to the feeder, the best thing to put in there is whole peanuts. The squirrels will try to take all of the peanuts, so we sometimes play a trick on them and grease the pole. It's fun to watch the squirrels try to climb the pole and then slide down.

BUTTERFLIES

We camped at a park where the roadside was bright orange with butterfly milkweed flowers. The flowers are beautiful, and so are all of the monarch butterflies they attract. After that, we planted butterfly milkweed at home. The tithonia plant we grew one year reached 8 feet high, and we counted up to 10 monarch butterflies at a time on the blossoms in late summer.

The other thing we grow that attracts butterflies is the herb dill. It seeds itself everywhere, so it's not a lot of work to plant. Dill attracts black swallowtail butterflies. We find their caterpillars on the dill. (See Countertop Caterpillars, page 50.)

MILKWEED
IS FUN FOR
KIDS, TOO!

A Sweet Thing to Do Together

Our friends Owen and Jack keep bees with their dad, Tom. Their bees turn flower nectar into sweet, yummy honey. Jack says his friends were creeped out when he first started working with the bees. Owen explains, "It's the most commonly misunderstood insect. Kids say, 'Hey, it's a bee,' when it's a wasp or hornet or yellow jacket that's buzzing them." Jack and Owen were scared of getting stung when they first started, but honeybees are not aggressive. "Even if they do sting, it doesn't hurt that much and it's worse for the bee — it dies!" says Owen.

Next to eating the honey, Jack's favorite part of beekeeping is using the bee smoker. He explains how he squeezes the bellows on a special smoker to puff smoke on the bees to make them sleepy and less likely to sting. Owen likes to help remove the wooden frames that the bees cover with honey-filled wax cells called honeycomb. Because of all the wax, the frames often stick to the hive, so he pries them out with a hive tool, which looks like a mini crowbar.

The process of harvesting honey is called *extracting*. Jack and Owen say they wear old clothes for this because they usually get pretty sticky. They use a special tool to shave off the end of the comb to let out the honey that is sealed inside the cells. Then the

frame goes into a machine called an *extractor* that swirls it around very fast and all the honey leaks out. It smells super sweet.

I Met the Bees!

"You'll never forget the first time you reach into that first colony," Tom told me. At first he was nervous, but now he wears shorts to work with the bees! "Bees only sting to protect the hive. If someone ripped the roof off your house and moved your mom around, you could imagine how a bee must feel." He says that the only time he gets stung is if he works with his bees at the wrong time, like when they are stressed by bad weather.

I didn't get stung either! I put on a bee veil, which is a net you wear over your head to keep away the bees.

Then, while Tom opened up the hive to check how the bees were doing, I used the smoker to give a few little puffs of smoke.

We watched bees come and go for a while. They didn't seem too worried about us being there. Lots of them had sacs of pollen on their back legs.

I asked Tom how to tell honeybees from other bugs that look like bees. "A yellow jacket has much brighter yellow stripes on its abdomen," he told me. Honeybees are generally more of a golden color and they're fuzzier. Honeybees want nectar, so they aren't interested in flying around your head. You won't find honeybees buzzing around picnics and garbage pails because they aren't interested in those sorts of things. If you're getting buzzed, it's probably yellow jackets.

YELLOW JACKET   WASP   BUMBLE BEE   HONEY BEE

BUILD A BUG GARDEN

There are lots of bugs to hunt for in gardens. Some are pests that feed on plants. Aphids are pests because they can damage or kill plants by sucking sap. Other bugs eat leaves, damage fruit, or attack roots. But there are lots of good bugs that you can hunt for, too. Some control bad bugs, some pollinate flowers, and some are good for the soil. (See pages 36 to 55 for more about bugs.)

Lots of bugs live under logs, rocks, or bricks. Keaton upsets Dad by lifting up flat rocks and logs that Dad has put around the edge of gardens. Dad doesn't like having to tidy up flipped-over rocks and logs that crush his plants. But these spots are great for bug hunting. Keaton finds centipedes, slugs, ants, and more.

Not sure why to look for bugs? It's fun hunting for things. They are neat to look at. And there are interesting things to do with them, too, like snail races. One day Keaton picked up more than 20 snails while we walked home from school, and we had snail races when we got home.

Here are some ideas for making bug habitats in the garden.

IDEAS FOR BUG HABITATS

LOGS. We keep logs in the backyard for our woodstove. They are always a good place for finding bugs. When we lift them up, we see slugs, ants, and centipedes.

ROCKS. Same as the logs above.

BUNDLES OF BRANCHES. Dad has a friend who doesn't like earwigs and catches them in bundles of branches that still have leaves on them. The earwigs crawl inside overnight, and when he shakes out the bundle in the morning, it's full of earwigs.

GRASS. If you have more lawn than garden, you can still find bugs! We catch crickets in late summer. And we hunt for the small white lawn moths and see who can catch the most.

WATER. Bugs need water, too, and we sometimes see them land in our birdbath for a drink.

STRAW AND HOLLOW STEMS. If you have old plant stems that are hollow, tie them in a bundle and see if you can attract solitary bees. (See Solitary Bees, page 54.)

UNCUT GRASS. We leave a patch of grass at the back of the yard unmowed all summer. It's a great place to hunt for grasshoppers, crickets, ladybugs, and solitary bees (and unwanted bugs, too, like fire ants!).

PICKING
RED
CURRANTS

BACKYARD FRUIT PLANTS

I love to go to orchards to pick apricots, plums, peaches, pears, and apples. You can't beat the wagon rides and climbing up ladders! But you don't need to have orchard-sized trees to get fruit in your garden. There are smaller (and easier) ways to get fruit. Here are some I love.

BLACKBERRIES. I remember a long stretch of chain-link fence at Nana Joanne and Papa Bob's house with clusters of blackberries all along it, some in sight, some hiding under leaves. Dad planted those blackberries when he was a kid. My brothers and I had full mouths and purple stains on our faces after we visited the fence. If you plant blackberries, get a thornless variety!

MELONS. You can grow them in the garden or in large pots. We grow ours in pots on the garage roof. Just watch out because the vines grow like crazy. Give them lots of space. You can even grow them up a trellis or over a tunnel!

GROUND-CHERRIES. This is my favorite backyard fruit. They grow in the garden or in pots. They even reseed themselves in the garden if you leave some of the fruit on the ground. I love peeling off the papery husk.

CAPE GOOSEBERRIES. These are a cousin to ground-cherries, except they take longer to ripen. But they are worth it. The fruit is a little bit bigger and has a tangier flavor.

HONEYBERRIES. These knee-high bushes produce long, corn-kernel-sized blue fruit early in the year. I love them, but so do the birds, so I have to pick every day if I want any.

SERVICEBERRIES (also known as June-berries). Serviceberries grow in so many of the parks and gardens here in Toronto that we can go for a walk and have a feast, but you can grow them in your yard, too.

They are sweet and look almost like blueberries. There are a few different types, some bigger, some smaller, some with more delicious fruit.

NANKING CHERRIES. This is a bush with bright red fruit that tastes like mini sour cherries. It reseeds itself, so we started a cherry hedge with all of the little seedlings.

NASTURTIUM

Nasturtium flowers are a bit spicy and peppery. Be sure to check for bugs before popping them in your mouth, though. One time Dad took a salad with nasturtium flowers to work. He added some dressing and left for a minute, and when he came back, he had oil-and-vinegar-covered aphids marching all over his salad!

Bachelor's button is an annual that we grow for bouquets. It has edible petals.

FLOWERS THAT LOOK, SMELL, AND TASTE GOOD

A lot of people are surprised by the idea of eating flowers. I like to get my friends to taste and smell things in my herb garden, like chives. Chives are in the onion family. Usually people just use the leaves, but we pick the purple flowers and eat them right in the garden or use them to decorate a plate of vegetables. We sometimes chomp on dill flowers. Oregano and thyme flowers are really small but we like to eat them, too.

BACHELOR'S BUTTON

Tips from a Flower-Eating Expert

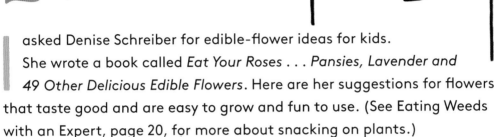

asked Denise Schreiber for edible-flower ideas for kids. She wrote a book called *Eat Your Roses . . . Pansies, Lavender and 49 Other Delicious Edible Flowers*. Here are her suggestions for flowers that taste good and are easy to grow and fun to use. (See Eating Weeds with an Expert, page 20, for more about snacking on plants.)

LAVENDER. "Lavender is really popular," says Denise, "and lavender and blueberries is a match made in heaven." Lavender goes well with sweet things, and that's good for kids. She suggests adding it to preserves or fruit sauces and then warming them up a bit before pouring over pancakes.

BEE BALM. Bee balm is great for attracting hummingbirds, but people like it, too. It's in the mint family. Try a few flowers floating in a glass of lemonade. And if you love fruit, Denise suggests chopping up some bee balm flowers and mint leaves, mixing them with lime juice, and pouring it over fruit salad – yum!

ROSES. Denise takes rose petals, removes the bitter white part at the end, and then cuts them up and mixes them with pitted black cherries. For dessert, sprinkle some chopped rose petals on ice cream.

NASTURTIUMS. Denise adds a layer of nasturtium flowers when she makes her vegetarian lasagna!

SMALL SURPRISES

We've talked about giant vegetables (see A Giant's Garden, page 76). Any of those giant veggie plants are cool plants to grow on their own. But vegetable size doesn't just mean really big stuff. Small plants (or plants that give small veggies) can be fun, too. Here are a few vegetable plants that have something tiny about them.

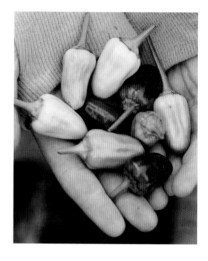

MOUSE MELONS

(also called Mexican sour gherkins or cucamelons) look like tiny watermelons about the size of your thumbnail. They grow on a vine and taste like crunchy mini cucumbers. It's an adventure hunting for mouse melons under the leaves of the vine. My brothers and I like to pack them in our lunches to take to school.

CURRANT TOMATOES

are tiny, smaller than marbles. The plants themselves grow to be big, so give them room when you plant them. The harvest isn't small, though: I can pick 100 to 200 tomatoes every two or three days!

TINY PEPPERS

are cute and tasty. Dad grows a lot of hot peppers that are small. I like to grow small, skinny sweet peppers that are about the size of a glue stick. I love the variety called 'Tequila Sunrise', which has yummy 6-inch peppers! They're great for picnics.

MOUSE
MELONS

BALSAM
SEEDPODS

DELIGHTFUL DISCOVERIES

When we hike in the woods in the fall, I look for an orange flower called jewelweed that has exploding seedpods. I love it. It was such a surprise the first time that I touched this seedpod and it blew out seeds in all directions! We grow another plant with exploding seedpods in our garden. Balsam seedpods, like jewelweed, get plumper and plumper. One day, with just a light touch, they spring apart and the seeds go flying. It's super fun. Balsam is an annual that Dad remembers from his grandmother's garden — an old-fashioned plant that you don't always find at garden centers. But it is easy to grow from seed and reseeds itself!

THERE ARE A LOT OF WAYS PLANTS CAN SURPRISE US.
Here are a few ideas for your garden.

TOUCH

The silver maple tree in our backyard drops tons of maple keys. If you collect them when they are young enough, the seed has not formed and the plump end is full of liquid. I point them at my brothers and ready, aim, fire! A press in the right spot, and they squirt liquid.

TASTE

For sure one of the weirdest things I've tasted is the flowers of the toothache plant, which is also called Szechuan buttons. The small yellow flowers are a bit spicy at first, and after a few seconds your tongue starts to tingle and get a bit numb. It's really neat, but you might want to warn your friends about this surprise before getting them to taste it!

SMELL

I am still waiting for this surprise to work, but when it does, it will be a good one. I have a voodoo lily bulb. So far it has only grown leaves. But when it grows a flower, I'll sneak it into the house, and watch out, Mom and Dad! They'll have to pinch their noses because voodoo lily flowers look neat and smell gross, like something rotten.

SIGHT

When you dig up roots of the wildflower blood-root and break a piece, a red liquid drips out. Then you understand the name! (Don't get the sap in your mouth, though, and wash your hands after handling it — it can be poisonous if you swallow it.)

TOUCH & TASTE

I love the litchi tomato. It has little red fruits that are so sweet and juicy, a bit like lychee fruit. But the plant is super spiky and will prickle you if you're not careful.

SIGHT & TASTE

If you let rat-tailed radishes go to seed, they make long, weird-looking pointed seedpods. What's neat is that the seedpods are crunchy, mild, and delicious.

SHAPE

Want forked and multi-rooted carrots? Just grow them in rocky soil! When the tip of the root hits a pebble, carrots sometimes split and twist.

FROG'S BELLY!

Surprising Sedum

For Papa Bob's specialty, you need some sedum, a plant that he called frog's belly when he was a kid. 'Autumn Joy' is a common variety of this plant. Squeeze the leaf between your thumb and finger all over so that you soften it, but be careful not to break the skin. Then, very carefully, squeeze sideways to loosen the skin on the top and bottom of the leaf. If you don't break the skin, you can blow up the leaf like a little balloon (or like a frog's belly) and pop it!

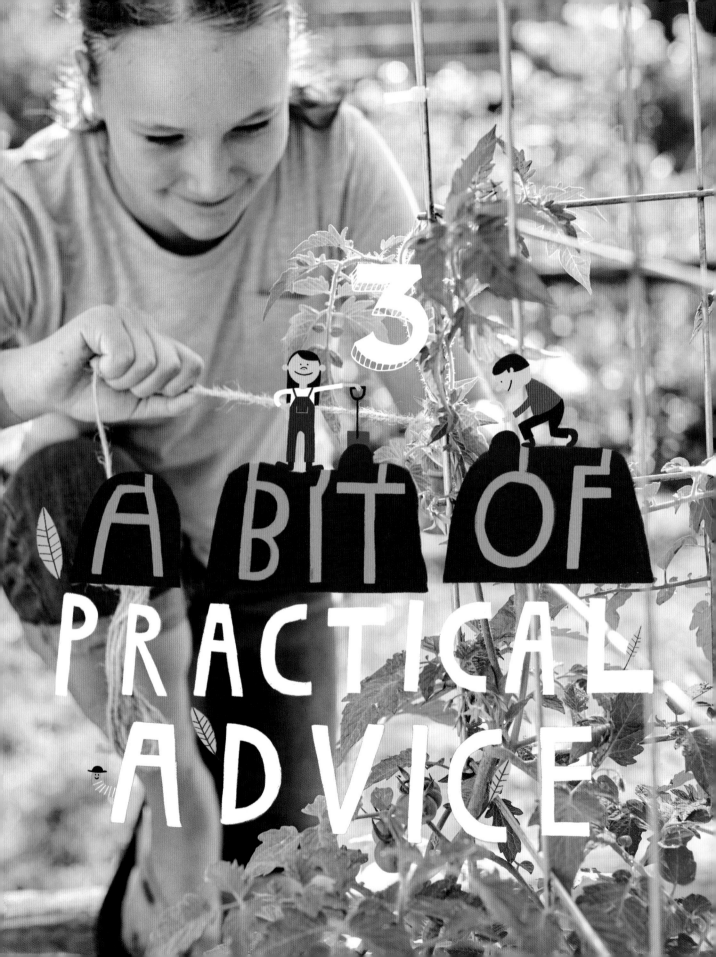

3

A BIT OF PRACTICAL ADVICE

YOU NEED A GARDEN OF YOUR OWN.

Think about your interests and have an idea of what you want to try to grow. To find a space, maybe you can take over an existing garden from your parents or maybe you'll have to make a new one. I did both. I took over a lot of Dad's garden for my herbs and tomatoes. But when I needed more space, we made a raised-bed garden as well as a container garden on the garage roof.

MAKING A NEW GARDEN

If you are making a new garden, you want good, loose soil that is not full of grass or other roots. Here are things we've tried that work.

GROW IN POTS. This is a super-easy way to start. You can grow many different plants in large pots or containers. Read the section on self-watering pots (page 31). If you do this, you can get really great results!

DIG OUT A PATCH OF GRASS. We've made some gardens by digging out the grass. Use a spade to chop the grass from underneath and peel back the grass from the soil like you peel the skin from a banana. Then dig down a few inches to loosen the soil.

MAKE A SIMPLE RAISED BED. If you don't want to remove grass, the easiest way to make a garden is just pile 6 or more inches of soil on top of the grass to make a raised bed. (Cut the grass short first.) If you put down less soil than that, the grass will eventually grow right through. It'll grow up around the edges anyway, but you can just cut it back or dig it out.

Dig out perennial weeds like dandelions, thistles, and quack grass first, because they will grow through a layer of soil. We've made a couple of raised beds this way. The good thing about raised beds is that the soil dries out and warms up more quickly in the spring.

EVEN BETTER: USE CARDBOARD. Another way to make a raised bed is by putting flattened cardboard boxes in sheets over the grass, then piling 6 to 8 inches of soil and compost on the cardboard. The grass dies after a few weeks, and the cardboard breaks down into the soil.

You can plant seeds and seedlings right away, while the grass is still alive, because there's enough soil on top for the roots to start growing. Just don't plant anything with a long taproot, like carrots, during the first season, before the cardboard breaks down.

OR BUILD A BOX. Some gardeners build a frame to hold the soil in place. You don't need to do this when you raise the soil only a few inches. But Dad and I did this for a bed where we wanted to raise the soil by more than a foot and include a liner so that the roots of my tomato plants wouldn't meet their arch enemy . . . the roots of the black walnut tree.

You can also make a frame like this if you're creating a garden on top of pavement or really compacted soil.

STARTING SEEDS INDOORS

Every year I buy some plants already growing in pots, but I also love growing plants from seed. There are more choices with seed. Not all plants can be started indoors, but some vegetables and flowers do better by getting a head start in your house. And it's really exciting to watch seeds grow into plants.

Gardening books and seed packages often tell you how many weeks before the last frost to start your seeds. What that means is that you take the last frost date in your area (you can find that online) and count backward. Our last frost date is usually around May 10, so I start my tomatoes seeds indoors, under bright lights, eight weeks before that, or March 15.

Fill small pots or seed flats most of the way with potting soil, put a few seeds in each pot, and cover with a thin layer of potting soil. Don't bury the seeds halfway down the pot! That's too deep.

Keep the soil moist until the seeds sprout. When plants are small, they can die easily if they get too much or too little water. Water them regularly and check for bugs. Once the seedlings are an inch or so high, use small scissors to carefully snip off all but one or two of the largest ones per pot. Too many seedlings all crowded together won't grow strong roots.

Once there's no more risk of frost, I move the seedlings to the garden.

SOW.
This is another word for planting seeds.

SEEDLING.
A young plant that has sprouted from a seed and has a few leaves.

LAST FROST DATE.
The last day that a frost usually happens in your area in spring.

SOWING SEEDS OUTSIDE

Sometimes there's no point starting seeds indoors. Plants that grow quickly might get too big indoors, and other ones don't like to be transplanted. For example, cucumber plants grow very quickly and take a lot of space. Since they do fine being planted straight in the garden, I don't start them indoors.

Some seeds, like carrots and peas, can be planted directly in the garden really early so there isn't a reason to grow them inside.

There isn't one right way to plant seeds. I find grown-ups like rows, but I usually plant my carrots in squares. I sprinkle the seed right on the soil, and then use a hand rake to mix it in with the top half inch of soil.

One rule is don't squish them all together. Plants need room to grow. Follow the directions on the seed packet. Most seeds need just a little bit of soil to cover them.

PLANTING OUTSIDE

Moving a seedling or grown plant to a new place is called *transplanting*. It can be planting a potted plant in the garden or moving a plant from one place in the garden to another. Before you move seedlings outside, though, you need to harden them off, which means getting them used to being outside in bright light, colder weather, and wind. You do this by putting the plants out for a little bit each day, starting in a shady spot so they don't get sunburned.

HARDEN OFF.
The way you get a plant used to being outside in bright light, colder weather, and wind. You do this by putting the plants out for a little bit each day, starting in a shady spot.

TRANSPLANT.
To move a plant. It can be from one pot to a bigger pot, or from a pot into the garden. It can also mean to move a plant from one place in the garden to another.

HERE ARE SOME TRANSPLANTING TIPS:

DIG A GOOD HOLE. Loosen the soil and dig a hole about the same depth as the pot, but a bit bigger all around to give the roots room to grow.

POP OUT THE PLANT. Before you pull your plant out of the pot, bang the pot gently on the ground or run an old butter knife around the inside to loosen the roots. You don't want to pull out the plant and leave most of the roots behind!

FILL IN THE HOLE. Put the plant in the hole and fill in around it with dirt. Press the soil down, but not too hard — you don't want to damage the roots.

WATER A LOT. Newly planted seedlings and plants need extra water, so don't forget them after the first couple of times.

125

CARING FOR YOUR GARDEN

Different plants and different types of gardens need different amounts of care. Even the sort of gardener that you are affects how much care the garden needs. For example, Dad is more worried about weeds than I am! Here are things to remember so you can take good care of your garden.

WATER. Believe me, the right amount of water makes a huge difference. Usually the problem is not enough water. After we set up planters with irrigation so that our plants were never thirsty, we had amazing results.

SUPPORT. Some plants need to be held up. I tie my tomatoes to poles or grow them in metal cages. It's important to keep checking and tying them up as they grow taller. Other plants that need staking are ones that grow on vines, like cucumbers and pole beans. Some tall flowers will flop over if you don't stake them.

WEEDS. Weeds steal water and space from your plants. Weed more often when plants are small, when they can't compete as well with weeds. Once they're big, they can compete better and you don't have to worry as much about weeding.

CRITTERS. Watch for bugs attacking your plants. Remember that some bugs are good. (See Creeping Crawling Critters, page 36.)

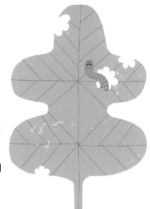

KEEP PLANTING. Not all plants grow at the same time. Others might not do well in the spot where you put them. Just keep planting. When aphids ruin my nasturtiums, I plant something else like fast-growing calendula seeds. Lettuce just doesn't last all summer, so I have more lettuce plants or lettuce seed ready to replace it. When we harvest garlic in July, we replant the patch with a late crop of beans or rapini, which is a bit like broccoli.

HARVEST. After all of your hard work, it's important to harvest fruits and vegetables when they are ripe. Sometimes things are ready all of a sudden and you have to pick a lot at once.

127

MAKING MORE PLANTS

Making more plants is known as *propagation*. I already talked about growing plants from seeds, my favorite way to propagate new plants. I love growing from seed so much that I have a shoe box filled with envelopes full of seed! But there are other ways to propagate plants, including taking cuttings, dividing, layering, and grafting.

CUTTINGS. With some types of plants, you can take a piece of stem (a cutting), put it in water or in soil, and it grows roots and becomes a new plant. For most plants you need to cut about 6 inches off. Pull off the bottom leaves before putting it in water.

DIVIDING. Many plants that grow in clumps can be divided to make more plants. When my clump of chives gets big enough, I just dig through it with a spade to divide it into two plants.

LAYERING. Layering is how Dad and I make more currant and black-berry plants. We bury a low branch, covering it with a bit of soil, and then put a rock on top to hold it down. After a while, the buried branch grows its own roots.

Then you can cut off the low branch from the main plant and you have a new plant with its own roots.

I called John Bagnasco at SuperNaturals Grafted Vegetables, who does a lot of work with grafted vegetables. John's company does something else cool with tomatoes. Tomatoes and potatoes are closely related, so they can be grafted, meaning you can harvest tomatoes and potatoes from one plant!

Last year I grew one of John's Ketchup 'n' Fries, which is a graft of a potato root with a tomato plant on top! It's fun for kids because it grows quickly and the tomato variety they use is the world's sweetest tomato, called 'Sweet Aperitif.'

GRAFTING
is when you take pieces of two different but related plants and join them together. It's often done with fruit trees.

ROOTS.
The potatoes are the roots of the tomatoes!

Extend Your Growing Season

I want a greenhouse so badly (to grow more tomatoes, of course)! The next best thing is a cold frame, which is like a low mini greenhouse. You can use a cold frame in the spring to start seeds earlier or harden seedlings off before planting them. In the fall, it lets you protect potted plants from frost or keep cool-weather crops, like kale, spinach, chard, and parsley, going longer.

It's easy to make a temporary one with some straw bales and an old window or sheet of thick, clear plastic to put on top. All you do is arrange the bales in a square, leaving an open space in the middle where you can put your seedlings. For an existing crop, arrange the bales around the plants. You can leave the top off when it's warm and sunny, but don't forget to cover them up at night to protect against frost.

Checking out tomato plants with Linda Crago

The Greatness of Greenhouses

Greenhouses capture energy from the sun and make a nice warm place for plants to grow in cool weather. The greenhouse covering, which is usually glass or clear plastic, holds in the heat. Think of how hot a car in the sun can get when the windows are closed: the sunlight goes in and warms things up. You can start seeds and protect young plants in a greenhouse, so it gives you a longer growing season.

My friend Linda Crago grows amazing types of tomatoes. When I visited her in May, it was cool enough outside that we needed coats. But inside her green-house, where her tomato seedlings were growing, it was toasty warm.

A greenhouse can get super hot inside when the days are long and the sun is bright, so at certain times of year, greenhouse growers might paint whitewash (a thin paint) on the glass. It keeps out some of the sunlight, so that the greenhouse is less bright and less hot. When fall comes and the light is less strong, the whitewash is washed off.

COLD FRAME COMPANIONS

LETTUCE

CARROTS

BEETS

KALE

CHARD

4

FALL AND WINTER GARDEN FUN

WE NORMALLY HAVE SNOWY WINTERS

in Toronto, with frost starting in late October. The annual plants in my garden die with the cold, and the perennials die back and *go dormant* (sleep) for winter. There are a few plants Dad and I take into the house as houseplants. We usually have some geraniums in our dining room window. They look nice during winter. We put a few of my special herbs in pots and store them in the garage, where they are protected from the cold. By now I have saved tomato seeds and seeds from other special plants.

There are some seeds I don't save but just sprinkle on the garden soil in the fall. I do this with dill, lettuce, and sunflowers.

Even though most of the plants in the garden are done for the year, I still hang out outside and enjoy my garden. Here are some ways to enjoy the outdoors even if most of your plants are finished for the year.

SO COLD

133

SPRING CLEANING IN THE FALL

LEAF COMPOST

If there are just a few tree leaves on your garden, you can leave them for the worms. But if you have a thick layer of leaves, rake them up and compost them.

Our big maple tree drops lots of leaves. We rake them into piles for jumping into. We sometimes rake leaves into rows to make the walls of pretend buildings. After a while, we have a whole street, and the wagon is our car!

When we're done playing, we put the leaves in the composter. If we can't fit them all in, we jump on them to pack them down, and that's fun, too! After a year, the leaves turn into compost and we add it back to the soil in our gardens.

Cleaning up the garden is way more fun than cleaning up your room! To clean up the garden, you harvest the last of your crops, pull out dead plants, trim other plants, and get things ready for spring. Some plants, like tomatoes and basil, die after the first frost, so I clean out those beds, but I leave other things that are still growing, like dill and oregano.

The dead plants go onto the compost pile, where they break down and turn into compost that I add back onto the garden in a year.

THINK SOIL

Once the growing season is over, we dig the soil in our vegetable gardens so that it's ready for planting in the spring. Loosening up the soil makes starting vegetable seeds like beets and carrots directly in the garden much easier. It's best to do this in the fall because sometimes the soil is too wet in the spring.

We don't mulch our vegetable gardens in the fall because we want the soil to warm up quickly in the spring. Mulch insulates soil, which keeps it cooler in the spring.

But we do put mulch on gardens with perennial flowers because we are not in a hurry to plant there in the spring, and the mulch protects the plants over the winter. We mulch with composted leaves from the previous year or old straw. Both of these are good for the soil. As they break down, they add organic matter to the soil.

PLANT FOR NEXT YEAR

Garlic grows best when you plant it in the fall instead of the spring. We plant garlic every fall after we dig up the soil in the vegetable garden.

First, we take the papery skin off of the garlic bulb. Then we separate the garlic bulb into sections, called *cloves*. It's like peeling and dividing an orange.

Push each clove of garlic into the soil with the top (the pointy part) facing up and cover it up. Don't forget to mark the rows!

Plant garlic in fall and harvest it partway through the summer!

Sprout a Snack

If you want to practice growing seeds with something easy, try sprouting dried seeds from the kitchen! The grocery store sells dried peas, lentils, and beans for cooking. In winter we grow the dried seeds into little plants and eat them. Some people call them *microgreens*.

IT'S REALLY EASY TO GROW YOUR OWN.

1. Soak the dried seeds overnight.
After they soak, they grow more quickly. While they're soaking, find something to grow them on: a pie plate or a large, low-sided container from the recycling bin.

2. Put a layer of potting soil on the plate, and sprinkle the soaked seeds thickly over the soil. (We don't even cover the seeds with soil.)

3. Put the plate on a sunny counter and wait a few days. If it's warm, you'll sometimes see little roots start to poke out of the seeds within a couple of days. Water the soil if it gets dry, but don't keep it constantly wet — just moist.

4. When the plants are 2 or 3 inches high, cut them off with scissors and eat them.

LENTIL SPROUTS

CHICK PEA SPROUTS

ENJOY YOUR GARDEN WITH FRIENDS

A garden is a fun place to hang out, and we like to invite our friends to play with us in ours. Every fall we have an apple cider–making party where we get out our cider press and spend the day pressing apples and being with friends.

If our big apple tree has apples, we use some of them for the cider. And we always gather lots of apples from orchards. I love picking apples! We make enough cider to freeze and drink all year. We make it an all-day event with a barbeque.

In addition to making cider, we hang apples from a tree and try to take bites without using our hands. You'd be surprised how hard it is! We float a bunch of apples in a tub and bob for apples. We climb trees and play tag. Everyone goes home with fresh cider that they helped make.

But you don't need an orchard or a cider press to have a fall party. You can invite friends over for a harvest party and make pizza or pasta sauce from your pickings. Have your friends help you build a straw-bale fort or go bug hunting.

WATCH YOUR JACK-O'-LANTERNS!

We cook and freeze lots of pumpkin in the fall so we can have pumpkin pie and pumpkin muffins all year. We carve lots of jack-o'-lanterns, too, with funny faces! After Halloween we move some of our jack-o'-lanterns to the garden, where we can watch them from the house as they rot and get eaten by squirrels.

It's neat to watch the pumpkins slowly rot. First they sag around the holes in the faces. Then the top falls into the pumpkin. They look a bit like wrinkled old people. Eventually they become slimy blobs and then flat pancakes of dried rind. By spring they are just spots on the soil.

MALE

FEMALE

CARDINALS

RED-TAILED HAWK

BIRD-WATCHING

In winter we put out seed and suet for birds. The birds are amazing to watch. We get nuthatches, woodpeckers, sparrows, finches, juncos, blue jays, cardinals — and even an occasional hawk in our city backyard.

One day Keaton saw something come down quickly from the sky and feathers flying. He ran over and scared away a hawk that had attacked a pigeon. He found the pigeon on the ground, and it was still alive, so we put it in a box with water and food. It was a racing pigeon, with a metal identification band on its leg. We contacted the owner, who said that he had released his pigeon more than 50 miles from our house and it was only partway home.

BIRD FEEDERS

BIRDHOUSE

SUET FEEDER

BIRDHOUSES

As well as bird feeders, we have birdhouses. Sometimes we cover the entrance holes in late winter so that house sparrows (which are an invasive bird species) don't nest in our birdhouses. That's because we really want wrens to live in them. We uncover the entrance holes after the sparrows make their nests in other places, but before the wrens nest. We haven't had any wrens yet, but we have had chickadees.

TRY HAND FEEDING

Near my cousin Jake's house, there's an amazing bird park. We hold out sunflower seeds on the palms of our hands and chickadees land right on us! We put seeds on our shoulders and the chickadees land there, too. We've also fed wild turkeys. We tried to feed blue jays by hand, but it didn't work. A bird-watcher we met explained that blue jays are very shy.

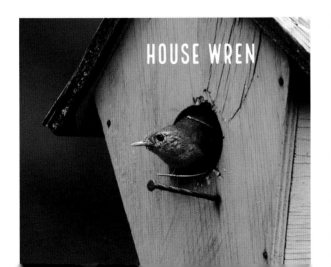

Plants in the House

I don't have a ton of houseplants because Dad hogs most of the windowsills. But growing flowers from bulbs doesn't take a lot of space. Growing bulbs inside is called *forcing* them. You do need to plan ahead and buy bulbs in the fall, when garden centers are selling them for planting in gardens. Bulbs that are good for forcing include crocus, hyacinth, dwarf iris, tulip, daffodil, and grape hyacinth. I love hyacinths because they smell so amazing.

Pot Them Up

Plant your bulbs in pots in the fall, soon after you get them. Choose a pot that isn't too tall because tall, skinny pots can tip over easily. Make sure your pot has holes in it. Put an inch or two of potting soil in the bottom, put in a few bulbs, and cover them with potting soil. It's fun to have several pots with a mix of bulbs. Water the soil well, but don't make it too wet.

Keep Them Cool

Put the pots somewhere cool but not freezing (like the basement or garage) so that they can root. They don't need light at this point.

Make Them Bloom

In midwinter, when your bulbs have roots showing at the bottom of the pot or are starting to grow leaves, bring them into the light to grow and flower. After the flowers die back, you can plant the bulbs in your garden in the spring and see if they come up the next year.

Every year I love watching amaryllis bulbs. They are big bulbs the size of grapefruit. You often get them as a kit, with a pot and soil. All you have to do is plant the bulb in the pot, water it, and watch it grow. Nana Linda gave me a beautiful one that grew a plump stem with four big flowers, and then sent up a second stem with more flowers!

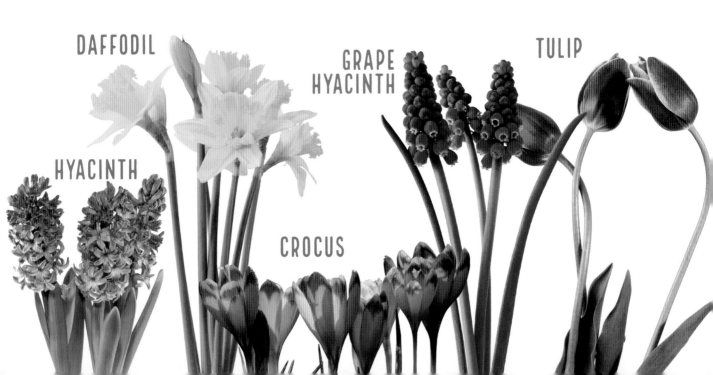

DAFFODIL

GRAPE HYACINTH

TULIP

HYACINTH

CROCUS

KEEP THINKING ABOUT NEXT YEAR!

When the weather isn't good for gardening, you can still dream of next year. I love going through seed catalogs in winter. Every year I find new tomato varieties to try. My goal is to have 100 varieties next year!

And I dream of new theme gardens to try, like my mint garden. Last winter as I looked through herb catalogs, I circled the cotton-candy mint, chocolate mint, and ginger mint. I was ready when spring came, and in the summer, yum, I was tasting different mints!

METRIC CONVERSIONS

To convert	to	multiply
teaspoons	milliliters	teaspoons by 4.93
gallons	liters	gallons by 3.785
inches	centimeters	inches by 2.54
feet	meters	feet by 0.3048
yards	meters	yards by 0.9144
miles	kilometers	miles by 1.609344
pounds	kilograms	pounds by 0.45

MY TOP ~~IQ~~ 130 TOMATOES
(THESE ARE THE ONES I GREW THIS YEAR)

- Allegheny Sunset
- Ananas Noire
- Aviuri
- Banana Legs
- Barry's Crazy Cherry
- Bedouin
- Beryl Beauty
- Better Bush
- Bi-Color Cherry
- Big Rainbow
- Black Cherry
- Black Krim
- Black Plum
- Black Prince
- Black Vernissage
- Blondkopfchen
- Blue Beauty
- Blue Berries
- Blue Green Zebra
- Blush
- Bosque Bumblebee
- Brad's Atomic Grape
- Brandywine
- Bush Beefsteak
- Carbon
- Casady's Folly
- Cherokee Green
- 'Cherokee Purple'
- Cherokee Tiger Black
- Copia
- Costoluto Genovese
- Coyote
- Cream Sausage
- Dancing With Smurfs
- Dark Galaxy
- Dark Italian
- Druzba
- Earl Of Edgecombe
- Emmy
- Federle
- Florentine Beauty
- Garden Peach
- Gezhante Buhrurkeel
- Glacial Zebra
- Great White
- 'Great White Blues'
- Green Doctors
- Green Grape
- Green Moldovan
- Green Sausage
- Green Tiger
- Green Vernissage
- Green Zebra
- Hillbilly
- House
- Indigo Apple
- Japanese Black Trifele
- Jersey Devil
- Jolie Coeur
- Kellogg's Breakfast
- Kelly Green
- Kookaburra Cackle
- Lebanese Mountain
- Lemon Drop
- Lemon Ice
- Longkeeper
- Lucky Tiger
- Marvel Stripe
- Matt's Wild Cherry
- Moonglow
- Morado
- Morelle de Balbis
- 'Mortgage Lifter'
- Nature's Riddle
- Oaxacan Pink
- Old German
- Orange Fleshed Purple Smudge
- Paul Robeson
- Persimmon
- Petit Chocolat
- Piedmont Pear
- Pilcer Vesy
- Pineapple
- Pink Accordion
- Pink Berkeley Tie-Dye
- Pink Bumble Bee
- Pink Passion
- Pink Ping Pong
- Pink Tiger
- Pink Zapotec Ribbed
- Plourde
- Plum Lemon
- Purple Bumble Bee
- 'Purple Calabash'
- Red Currant
- Red Fig
- Red Oxheart
- Reisetomate
- Riesentraube
- Royal Hillbilly
- Saint Pierre
- Santorini
- Serendipity Striped
- Sicilian Saucer
- SkyReacher
- Spike
- Striped Cavern
- Striped Stuffer
- Sub Arctic Plenty
- 'Sunrise Bumble Bee'
- Sunrise Sauce
- Sweet Apertif
- Tangella
- Tasmanian Chocolate
- Tiger Tom
- Tigerella
- Uluru Ochre
- Violet Jasper
- Wapsipinicon Peach
- Watermelon Beefsteak
- White Cherry
- Wild Fred
- Winter
- Yellow Brandywine
- Yellow Currant
- Yellow Fire
- Yellow Pear
- Yoder's German
- Yukon Quest